The Invisible Fist

Secret Ninja Techniques of Vanishing Without Leaving A Trace

Ashida Kim

DOJO *Press*

INVISIBLE FIST OF THE NINJA
copyright © 1998 Ashida Kim

ISBN 978-1-4357-8882-4

All rights reserved. This book may not be reproduced in any form whatsoever without written permission of the Author and Publisher except by newspaper or magazine reviews who wish to quote brief passages in connection for review. Books may be purchased in bulk at wholesale discounts for sales promotion, fund-raising, or educational purposes. Special editions can be created to specifications. Editorial, sales and distribution, rights and permissions inquiries should be addressed to:

DOJO Press
P.O. Box 209 Lake Alfred, FL 33850 USA
AshidaKim.com   DojoPress.com

"I cannot describe to you the indescribable, but I can teach you several by no means inconsiderable arts- invisibility, flying without wings, invulnerability to sword or serpent's fang- you know, that kind of thing.

"Here then is your syllabus of study. Seeking the mysterious portal, you must first provide yourself with the wherewithal to bribe the guards and render yourself invisible that you may slip through unnoticed. That sort of thing is not mastered in a day.

"Next you will have to learn to fly henceforth to the courts of Heaven, make your way to the central chamber, surprise Lord Lao at breakfast, snatch up his flask of golden elixir, slay those who will come running to rescue it, break down the walls of the sky-castle and return to Earth an immortal! A man of your determination has but to follow my course of instruction to be certain of success."

From the *Nei Pien of Ko Hung*, an ancient treatise on alchemy, medicine and religion 320.A.D.

Collector's History

The Invisible Fist was originally written and submitted for publication to Paladin Press in 1989. It was declined because by that time relations between Kim-Sensei and Paladin Press were strained. Kim having discovered several titles that had been re-named and were being sold without royalties being paid, and overseas sales that were completely unreported for many years.

In 1998 it was published by Citadel Press, after more than a year of "polishing" and their insistence that the chapter entitled Book of Fire be replaced for fear some moron would set himself on fire trying the Fire Breathing Dragon Technique.

Since then, Carol Publishing Group, the parent company of Citadel Press has declared bankruptcy. Although they remain in business and continue to sell Kim-Sensei's books such as *Secrets of the Ninja* in paperback edition through front companies like Berkeley Press without paying the author a nickel.

As part of the "liquidation" of Carol's assets, *Invisible Fist*, *Iron Body Ninja*, and the unfinished *Ninjitsu For Women* were sold, despite Kim's objections and in violation of his contract with Carol, to Kensington Publishing who have merely carried on under-reporting and using "accounting devices" to rob the author.

DOJO Press is the ONLY AUTHORIZEDDISTRIBUTOR OF ASHIDA KIM BOOKS AND TAPES, this edition has been retyped and reproduced from original photographs in its original format with Fire Breathing Dragon included, instead of the forced changes. Ashida Kim considers this book to be one of his best efforts to explain Ninjitsu, the only non-violent martial art known to man, and deeply regrets the delay in providing this information to the public.

-Editor 2001

Contents

Preface	6
Introduction: Invisibility as an Art	12
The BOOK OF EARTH "Grain of Sand in Eye Can Hide Mountain…"	21
The BOOK OF WATER "The Pool of the Subconscious…"	57
The BOOK OF FIRE "Fire Breathing Dragon Technique…"	79
The BOOK OF AIR "Power to Cloud Men's Minds…"	118
The BOOK OF WOOD	150
Postscript	184
The Sword the Does Not Kill	187

DOJO *Press*

Preface

Looked for, cannot be seen. Listened for, cannot be heard. Felt for, cannot be touched. The Invisible Fist gives no warning, nor can it be stopped. You cannot hide from it, nor can you escape it.

Why is this so?

Any decent self-defense class can teach one to draw up his courage in the face of danger, the better to execute one all-out, totally committed, do-or-die technique. This usually results in the mutually assured destruction of both combatants.

To strike the opponent without being struck in return is the essence of Boxing. Some martial arts teach that a punch must be so swift and return so quickly that it is faster than the human eye can follow as a method of being considered "invisible"

If the body can move faster than the eye, however, it can also react faster. The old magicians claim that the "hand is quicker than the eye" applies equally to defender and attacker. So, no matter how fast you are, no matter how many hours or years you may have spent training to react to an attack with an appropriate block, you still cannot block or hit what you cannot see. Thus, the true Invisible Fist would also be one that strikes from an unexpected angle. It gives no warning and cannot be deflected. One cannot hide from it because those who have the secret do not go around showing it off. If it is encountered, it is due to one's own bad karma in looking for a fight with a master.

Nor can one escape the wrath of the Invisible Fist, since it is brought upon oneself by bad conduct. In this way, those who would commit evil attract the very forces that will mete out appropriate justice to them. The Invisible Fist is merely one such tool.

That is why, at certain periods in history, those who practiced this art were known as the *Black Dragon Tong of Retribution*. Not because they went around like Robin Hood, "righting wrongs and punishing evil doers," But because they were simple humble people who were often mistaken for victims. If they could not escape, they were, and are today, quite capable of destroying any attacker in order to survive. Also being humble, knowing that the taking of a life does no one honor, they would accept no credit for such acts. They obeyed the ancient Samurai injunction to have the "power to kill and walk away" without any explanation being required long before it was instituted for that social class. This is because the followers of this Way are so inoffensive that at one time the founders thought themselves in such harmony with nature that they would limit the number of footsteps they made each day so as not to disturb the Earth with their presence. The rule is: First, do no harm; Second, never make a challenge; Third, never turn down a real challenge.

Bullies, muggers, rapists and the like often have a long history of crimes, violent or otherwise. So, when a criminal is found dead, it is frequently taken for granted that some old enemy must have caught up with him and extracted some measure of revenge. For surely, only one as brutal, ruthless and deadly as the villain himself could have overcome him.

This, however, is not necessarily so. What of the kind? The weak? The aged? Are they to have no defense except Force, which they are often ill inclined or unable to employ with enough skill or strength to be effective? Should they be armed, even with non-violent types of weaponry, which can be taken away and used by an attacker? Making a weapon as dangerous to the user as for the victim? Or, should they simply resign themselves to being sheep, preyed upon by the more aggressive and assertive wolves, fleeced and butchered at the whim of those less worthy, who contribute nothing to the welfare of the tribe and, in fact, greatly contribute to its downfall by their inappropriate behavior? No, they need not.

"What a piece of work is man…" asked Shakespeare in his classic play Hamlet. "In peace how noble and temperate, in war how terrifying…" All warfare is a matter of will. It is not the technique, the style, nor even the philosophy of the defender that determines the outcome. It is his Will, that gives him the stamina to continue until the opponent is exhausted and defeated.

When martial arts such as Karate, Kung Fu, and so on were first introduced to America, two claims were made about them; that *anyone* could overcome any attacker and could do so *without physical contact*.

Regardless of size, age, or infirmity, one need never again fear assault, because these fighting systems made it possible to control a fight long before it began, and, if the initiative was lost due to surprise attack, take it back from even a ferocious and aggressive enemy. BUT, all required the user to stand and fight.

Ninjitsu, the Invisible Fist, is the ONLY martial art that is not about fighting. It is about running away and hiding. It is about good health and longevity. It is about patience, because all true masters know that living well is the best revenge. Thus, it is by explaining the method whereby the promises made by those who would commercialize it are fulfilled.

All martial arts and their philosophies agree that the greatest warrior is the one who wins without fighting. In the classic martial arts film *Enter the Dragon*, the late Bruce Lee illustrated this principle when he confronted a brutish bully's challenge. He told this lout that his own style was the "art of fighting without fighting." But, he would need more room than the small ship they were on to demonstrate it properly. He thus enticed the bully to board a small boat so they could go to a nearby island.

Once the bully was in the lifeboat, Lee simply slipped the mooring line free and held him at his mercy by threatening to set him adrift in the turbulent seas. He had won without throwing a single punch. He had outwitted his opponent; fighting without fighting.

In the television series *Hanto Yo*, about the American Cheyenne Indian tribe, the mystic-warrior, the only one who dared ride a white horse into battle, the "shirt-man" and hero and beloved of the tribe, was the most adept at leading the enemy forces deep into the forest and away from his fleeing people. He single-handedly defeated the enemy by letting them wear themselves out chasing him. Once, when he fought on the plains, an eclipse took place while he was charging alone toward an attacking tribe- an example of synchronicity, harmony with the Universe. Just as playing hide-and-seek in the forest is an example of invisibility. This "mystic" occurrence so upset and terrified the opposing tribe that the battle was never fought and the war was called off. Yet, to be such a fearsome warrior, Hanto Yo spoke always of peace and harmony among the "human beings" as the Cheyenne tribe was known to call itself.

The Shaolin monks of ancient China were also known for their serenity and love of peace, even though they were trained to "fight like ten tigers." They saw it as their duty to defend China from foreign invaders. To that end, they launched the Boxer Rebellion in 1900. The members of the White Lotus Sect practiced ritualistic magic as a part of their traditional boxing art and placed such faith in their use of Iron Body Kung Fu that many believed themselves impervious even to bullets. They have long been recognized as masters of the martial arts and at the core of their study is breath control, non-violence, and self-knowledge. In fact, part of their credo reads, "When faced with imminent peril of life and limb, make no show of force. Rather, one should run away than fight."

Only when flight is no longer possible may one use Force to establish, maintain, or restore order. Even then, it is taught to "avoid rather than check; check rather than block; block rather than strike; strike rather than hurt; hurt rather than maim; maim rather than kill; kill rather than be killed. For all life is precious, nor can any be replaced."

The monks were each trained in a particular animal system of fighting depending on their body type and disposition, but all were taught meditation and the art of acting invisibly. These are the source of their great internal strength and the basis of their amazing powers. Through a series of tests and trials that were ritualized into a rite of passage into manhood they became mystic-warriors who could fight or disappear. The technique, however, was ancient long before it was incorporated into the Japanese *Shinobi-ryu* systems.

One of the earliest known tribes of ancient China was called the *Jain*. They were the greatest hunters and warriors of their era and are even spoken of highly by the famous anthropologist Joseph Campbell in his works on arcane religions. They were possessed of one great secret: they knew enough to build a fire and walk through the smoke to remove the scent of man from themselves before venturing into the woods for a hunt. Upon this ritual they based an entire philosophy of invisibility. They were Brothers of the Smoke and, like many later arts, ritualized the secrets of their clan into ceremonies. This included walking on hot coals, fire eating, smoking the pipe, and such philosophical concepts as being so in harmony with Nature that no force of man could harm them. They may yet exist. As the Invisible People, who can say from whence they came of if they have ever left or even if they are still among us.

What we do have of them is this system of fighting techniques divided into five elemental categories. In olden days it might take half a lifetime to master a single Shaolin system of fighting. The Invisible Fist is so simple it can be learned in a day. It is, without doubt, the single most effective self-defense form known to man. Just one of these basic techniques can make you the equal of any mugger, or even a well trained martial artist. Now you too can be one of the few, the proud, the Ninja, masters of the Invisible Fist.

INTRODUCTION:
Invisibility as an Art

Ninjitsu, contrary to popular belief, is not a system of unarmed combat or mastery of an array of martial arts weapons. It is not about fighting at all, it is about INVISIBILITY...

Every other martial art teaches that, "It is better to run away from a fight than to battle and have to injure someone." Then they spend the next two years teaching the student how to stand and fight. Ninjitsu teaches you how to prevail over even the most ferocious foe without physical contact and simply escape, leaving him alone in frustration.

When *Book of the Ninja* was published in 1980, it stated, "There is no magical technique to render oneself unseeable to the human eye." The basis for this being that all the Ninja methods of vanishing in front of the enemy rely on simple principles of ordinary stage magic, rather than mystic incantations.

Such techniques, however, do exist and can be learned through a series of specific exercises and tests devised by the venerable masters of the Pole Star School, circa 6000 B.C. recognized in China as the most ancient school of martial arts known to man. Furthermore, these methods are reserved only for those beyond the initiate or adept level of training.

The nature of those who teach the Secret Doctrine is to deny that it exists until all other methods have been studied, exhausted, and found lacking. Only then, when the student persists in his belief that there is more magic than simple tricks and mumbo-jumbo, only when he is ready to believe.

Only when he wonders what it all means instead of how it is done, THEN the secret is revealed.

These techniques are the basis for the Japanese Art of Invisibility known as Ninjitsu, the Silent Way. In them you will find many bits and pieces of others styles and systems. After all, there are only so many kicks, punches, throws, takedowns and so on. What differentiates one style from another is little more than a matter of hard or soft presentation and a focus on a particular sort of technique, a variety of combinations, poetic or military nomenclature, and strategy. All teach essentially the same lessons and all are part of the warrior quest. All possess some part of the Great Secret of Warriorship, because there are only five elements in combat and the same principles apply to the art of vanishing. Only the intent is different.

This set of techniques is but one of many. There is nothing new in magic, only new presentations of the same basic physical and chemical properties that have amused, entertained and amazed man for centuries. There are nine methods of the Black Dragon School given here. Derived from the Eight Mystic Trigrams that form the basis for the *I Ching*, the Chinese Book of Changes. These are divided into Five Elements, which is the foundation of Chinese medicine from antiquity to the present. The *dragon* represents mystical power. The adjunctive *black* indicates that it is a hidden, closed, or concealed system.

There are others who have pursued and employed the techniques of invisibility. The Rosicrucians, the followers of Gnosticism, the Kahuna, wizards, witches, and shamen throughout the ages have sought this mystical ability. Some vanish by rearranging the physical structure of their corporeal being so that light may pass unhindered through them. Thus, they become invisible.

Some disassemble themselves in an instant and reform elsewhere, safely out of harm's way. Then there are those who bend the very rays of light itself around themselves to form a shimmering cloud of obscurity that hides them from view. Finally, there are those with the power to place the idea of invisibility into the mind of the observer so that he refuses to see that which is clearly before his eyes. This is known as the Dragon Method of "clouding men's minds," and one means whereby practical invisibility may be achieved.

To that end, here are assembled the various techniques used by the Black Dragon Ninja for making an attacker blink, hesitate, flinch, turn away, or otherwise distract him from he who wishes to become in invisible; including methods that temporarily or permanently blind an opponent. Absent are the various tricks of remaining invisible, like hiding, and the methods of striking from ambush, which is a way of winning any conflict in a single devastating blow. These are considerations to be taken into account once invisibility has been achieved and are dealt with in other publications. The concern of this text is the ability to disappear.

The Art of Invisibility is divided into Five Elements:camouflage, concealment, cover, appearing, and vanishing. These equate quite nicely with the traditional Five Elements of Chinese medicine and philosophy, on which many martial arts are also based. It is a simple and effective method of categorizing a variety of techniques into easily defined groups so they can be remembered. This also allows for the inclusion of new techniques as they are developed or discovered. Thus, then system remains consistent and traditional, yet still dynamic and evolving. This method also makes it possible to compare systems that may, at first, seem widely disparate. The Five Elements can be mnemonically recalled at any time by using the fingers.

Earth is the little or pinky finger
Water is the ring or third finger
Fire is the middle finger
Air is the index finger
Wood is represented by the thumb.

Each represents a state of matter- solid, liquid, gaseous; and a type of energy- linear, circular, or spiral. Thus, even though such primitive systems are usually discredited by modern scientists as being merely examples of allegorical reasoning, such classification to illustrate the interaction of physical and chemical properties, altogether avoids the issue of whether matter and energy are two dissimilar states of being or are interchangeable. A question that has plagued modern scientific minds for decades.

To the ancients, such a question was meaningless. It was not important whether matter can be created or energy destroyed. What is important is how things interact. Nor were the ancients prone, as is so often the case in recorded history, to try to discover how things worked by dissecting them. Instead, they merely observed and noted cause and effect, and developed what today are called hypothetical constructs that could be tested and validated like modern laboratory experiments. The old ones called these "patterns," and had no need for vast, complicated texts to explain them. They had only a few simple "laws" that covered them all.

In keeping with the Five Element symbolism, this text is divided into five sections. This is the traditional way of presenting such material, on a scroll or scrolls, sometimes known as *tori-maki*, meaning "sacred writings." In the Hai Lung Ryu (Black Dragon School) there are many such arcane manuscripts, usually categorized by the element they are said to represent.

Each of the Five Elements interacts with the others, just as their symbolic names imply, and so represent the endless cycle of growth, change, and rebirth. Each also represents what modern scientists would call a state of matter.

For ages it was believed that matter existed in one of three states and that matter and energy could not be created or destroyed. This may well be true, but, what does it tell us about how these states interact?

The old Ninja Five Element Formula explains it all and includes even more than had been previously "discovered," such as the plasma energy level.

Earth is the most solid form of matter. It has weight and occupies space. Water is the liquid state of matter. The particles are not so tightly packed nor bound together in a shape. Air is the next most gaseous type of matter in which the particles are even more widely dispersed. Fire represents the plasma state of matter, a level of transition between what are called matter and energy only recently discovered by atomic science. Wood describes the three types of motion, linear, circular and spiral, in which these particles and their manifestations may engage; electromagnetic vibratory force acting in a circular motion about a linear axis. This is the Force.

So, everything is covered. From matter to non-matter and all degrees of vibratory existence and excitement in between, which determine the level of perception upon which they exist.

We who have studied and practice these arts have no fear they will be learned by anyone with criminal intent or deviant moral fiber. Such persons do not have the patience to advance slowly, step by step, through the long process of study and may even attempt advanced techniques without proper preparation or precaution, leading only to their demise.

One cannot learn how to be a "fire-breathing dragon" without first learning how to breathe properly. And, all war, indeed all life, is a matter of breath control.

This course of study is arranged in logical order for self-instruction. Each lesson is a building block for the next. We have found that when one studies in this manner, one advances at his own rate and level of interest and must actively participate in the course.

When one undertakes such an inner journey, one often returns "changed"- not in the sense that he is possessed of some new magical power, but rather that his level of spirituality and understanding have been raised and he has gained a new appreciation of life; and others will perceive this in your new demeanor.

Invisibility is a power man has strived for throughout the ages. Like flying, levitation, precognition, telepathy, healing and speaking with those who have passed on, it has fascinated and intrigued the great minds of sages, alchemists, and yogis as an expression of the ability to become so still you can see the workings of the universe and defend oneself through non-violence. After all, it takes two to make a fight. If only one is present, then he must eventually see that all anger is directed at the Self alone, by the Self alone. Frustration at the acts of others is a manifestation of ego, a projecting of one's own faults onto others. Likewise, all wounds are ultimately self-inflicted.

No one can see the future accurately. Only general trends, reflected by the Heavens or the seasons, give any real semblance of precognition. So, to anticipate the outcome of any future event is necessarily to build up an expectation that is unattainable. Regardless of whether we expect doom or gloom or roses or rainbows, the actual outcome of any event is never exactly as we had hoped or feared. Thus, humankind has for eons set itself up for endless disappointment and frustration.

Expect nothing! Judge nothing! Each morning, like a scholar at his first class, prepare a blank mind upon which the day may write. With this single act you can change the world. Or, at least your perception of it.

Most psychologists would agree that the perception of reality, either as a glorious world full of hope and opportunity or a dark and sinister place where virtue is often crushed by greed, is largely a matter of perspective, and have devised some clever tests to illustrate to their patients the fallacy of their thinking. One example being, "Is the glass half full or half empty?" The pessimist sees the glass half empty, perceiving only what has been lost or consumed. The optimist sees the glass half full, observing what remains.

The correct answer for a sage, or a Ninja, would be that the glass is too big for the amount of water it is intended to contain. Not a "smart-aleck" answer at all, although it might be seen as such by a researcher "expecting' one of the two answers he provided. Instead, what it illustrates is that the patient is capable of thinking, of reasoning, of seeing more than just two outcomes. Such is the purpose of such Buddhist *koans*- to make the student think! So, modern psychiatry has not invented anything new with this "test," and, in fact, as given in the above example, is not even aware of how to use the technique properly.

How much easier must it be then, for a martial art to lose sight of its past, its objectives, even its principles, if it remains only static, unchanging and limited. Ninjitsu is translated from the Japanese to mean, "the Silent Way." This is because those who practice it do not go about bragging of it to others, or even trying to share it with them, until such time as they themselves may ask. The Invisible Fist is not a "secret society." It is, however, a society with secrets.

Keep that thought before you as you study these techniques. Many of which are revealed here for the first time. Some are used by stage magicians even today. Others have strategic and tactical considerations. Some are pure fantasy. That is also part of what must be learned- that the historical martial trilogy of mind, body and spirit, like so many other things in the world, are merely symbols, code words for simple basic, ideas, crammed and distorted by the classical mess of rigid "traditionalism" that restricts normal growth and evolution.

Mind is memory, spirit is imagination, and body is touch; the test of Reality created by mind and spirit. Hallucinations can be seen, but not touched. Voices can be heard, but not touched. Tangible, repeatable, empirical experimental evidence is the only test of Reality on this Plane of Existence.

Remember that the human being is possessed of an automatic defense mechanism known clinically as the "fight-or-flight" adrenalin response. This is also seen in Nature and is a well documented fact. At this moment, we shall begin to associate this physio-chemical phenomenon that endows the body with tremendous strength, heightened awareness and lightning reflexes, toward the task of becoming invisible. In so doing, we assume responsibility for our actions and conscious control of the defensive aspect of this response and so we can program it with a type of behavior that has been proven through the centuries to be highly effective.

The "adrenal pump" is activated by fear. And, when one experiments with fear one must be prepared for the consequences. The "dark side" of the Self is always ready to engulf those who would use such power for personal gain or self-aggrandizement. But, it is only by making the inner journey, bathing in the pool of the subconscious and gazing into the mirrored, reflected image of the "dark self" or "shadow" that true understanding is possible. Therefore, do not step lightly upon the Moonlit Path of the Silent Way, for it will change your life. It is a road to self-knowledge and through that, knowledge of others. It is an inner Vision Quest, a puzzle wrapped in a mystery, surrounded by an enigma or our own creation. But, it can be done; and, is well worth the effort.

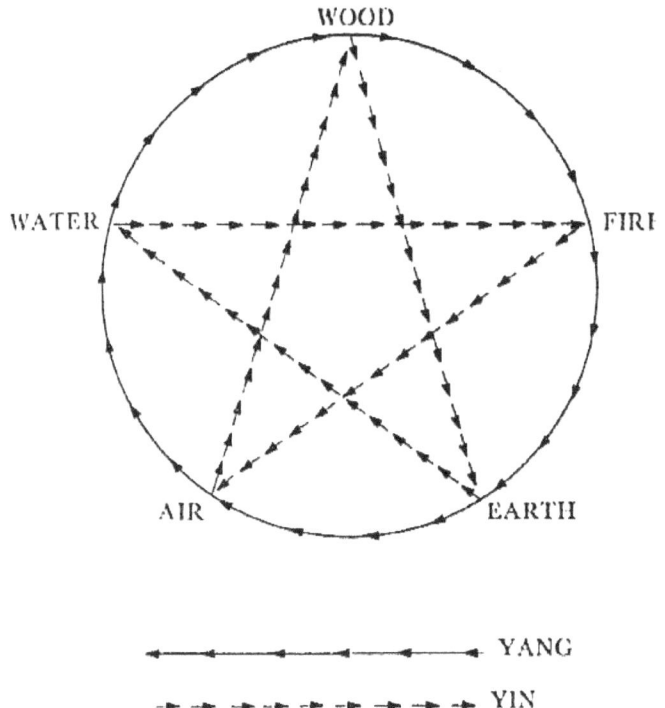

Diagram relationship of the Yin (destructive) Cycle and Yang (creative) Cycle of the Five Elements

The Book of EARTH

"Grain of sand in eye can hide mountain…"

-Sidney Toler as Charlie Chan, 1937

The first duty of any martial art worth its salt is to provide its students with an adequate means of self-defense. Most schools spend years helping students develop skills and moral outlook necessary for real competence in fighting. We begin, however, with a simple and effective technique that can be used by anyone, with no practice whatsoever.

Probably the most ancient technique for disabling an enemy is blinding him, temporarily or permanently. Perhaps the tactic that best serves to illustrate this point is the art of throwing dirt in the eyes of an opponent. In motion pictures this is sometimes done by the villain and is considered to be an unfair or dirty trick-

But, what is more unfair than being beaten to death?

In fact this method probably developed when a smaller combatant was thrown to the ground by a larger one and found his hands full of earth as a natural course of events and his rage and frustration. Hurling this virtually weightless substance at an on rushing foe might well have been a reflex or an act of desperation, unlikely to have any effect. Still, who can deflect a handful of sand? At the very least, the attacker will blink instinctively and provide an opportunity for the defender to escape.

This is where the Art of Invisibility begins.

Far from being futile, such a defense is the single most effective non-violent method or disappearing ever devised. Depending on the composition of the powder or dust used to blind an attacker, injury may range anywhere from momentary discomfort to permanent blindness.

BLACK EGGS

The ancient Ninja of the Black Dragon School carried their blinding powders in specially constructed containers ready for instant use. These were called *Hai Lan*, or "black eggs." They were made by poking a small hole in both ends of an egg and then blowing into the shell so that the contents are forced out the other end. In this way the raw egg could be extracted without breaking the shell. The egg would then be very fragile, so one had to be careful.

With a razor or sharp knife open one of the blowholes a bit more widely and plug the hole at the other end with a small bit of wax. Let the shell dry completely. Fill the eggshell with your secret blinding formula. Each *ryu* (school) had its own.

This may be the ash of a particular type of tree indigenous to the tribal area of the clan, finely ground bone chips, salt, dry bleach, beach sand, or any similar material. Exotic compounds included certain weeds and alkaloid plants that produce a sparkling effect when reacting with the water from tears. Various peppers can produce blindness; even the metal filings from a sharpened sword could be included to scratch the cornea and thereby inflict more permanent damage.

Seal the eggshell with homemade glue or wax. The Ninja of old had several formulae for this, but today commercially available adhesives are more than adequate. Once dry, the eggshell becomes a perfect container for a handful of dust and is easily hidden in the hand. It is too fragile to carry in a pocket, but, because of this fragility it will easily spill its contents just when needed.

The *Hai Lan* can be hardened somewhat by painting it with several thick coats of lacquer or black paint. A little bit of experimentation will determine how much is needed. You are now armed with one of the most ancient and secret of all Ninja weapons- the Black Egg.

SHADOW DUST

At this juncture a special word should be said about the practice of "hiding in the shadows." While this may seem to belong properly to the category of camouflage, it is also part of the manufacture of Black Eggs or Ninja Dust Bombs.

The Ninja discovered that the lighter the material that composed the contents of these eggs, the longer it was likely to hang in the air and be an effective barrier to vision. Some experimentation proved that ashes and dust were the two best substances to make a simple powder for this purpose.

Being frugal and not wishing to waste anything, the humble Ninja did not throw away the ashes from his fire, anymore than he discarded the contents of the egg. He ate that egg to give him strength and turned the shell into a weapon filled with those ashes. Likewise, in his housecleaning, scuttling about his dwelling, or busily sweeping as a servant to some lord, the Ninja was also collecting ammunition for his blinding powder devices. Since dust was often found in corners, under stairs, and above doorways, one engaged in cleaning would naturally become familiar with those places and so be better able to conceal himself in their shadows, should the need arise. Also, when watching an enemy in preparation for an ambush, collecting sand sifting dust or sand between the fingers serves to calm the mind by giving the hands something to do.

Thus, hiding in the shadows is more than just a technique of *Inpo* (the art of stealing in or hiding). It is also a meditation on stillness and silence and part of the practice for later skills that involve collecting and cultivating Qi, the vital life-force of the universe that surrounds and pervades all things.

THE CLOUD OF DUST

Two methods of delivering the Ninja Dust Bomb against an opponent present themselves automatically. One is to crush the egg in the hand and throw the contents into the enemy's face using any one of a great variety of flinging techniques, many of which are seen in *Shuriken-Jitsu*, named for the spikes and star shaped multi-pointed throwing blades for which the Ninja are famous. Range is, of course, limited. Owing to the lightness of the tiny particulate matter and missiles involved.

The practice method for this technique is to throw a dry washcloth at a head sized target or partner. This will fly about as well and as far as a handful of dust, and so provides good training and evaluation for the student without making a dusty or cloudy mess.

The third method is the basis for the myth that Ninja had grenades that exploded on impact and created a cloud of smoke in which they could vanish. Given the crude gunpowder of the era and the natural aversion to carrying something that might blow up in your pocket should you fall on it, the Ninja practiced throwing the dust bombs against the ceiling so that powder would rain down forming a curtain behind which they might disappear. To the untrained eye this has the same effect of throwing something on the floor and having it explode upward. Any ancient exploding devices to create smoke were necessarily were detonated by primitive fuses rather than impact.

Like many things that first seem amazing, when the explanation is known, they are quite simple. That is what makes it "magic."

The WITCH DOCTOR METHOD

This technique, Blowing Powder in the Enemy's Face, was used with great efficacy in the motion picture *The Serpent and the Rainbow* (1979). The subject dealt with Haitian voodoo and was based on the true adventure of a modern scientist researching the subject. The dust used by the Haitian witch doctors to subdue and paralyze their victims was a hallucinogenic mixed with a small amount of puffer fish poison that conducted the psychedelic directly through the skin of the victim.

Hold the powder filled eggshell concealed in the hollow of your hand. Move into effective range, established by a little practice beforehand. Or, let the enemy come within range as he advances aggressively. Crush the eggshell in your palm. The noise will attract the enemy's attention, it is one that is recognizable but unusual in combat. Thus, he hesitates to see where the sound came from. Watch his eyes. When he blinks or looks at your hand, he has lost the battle.

Immediately turn the palm up in the manner of a magician showing you a treasure he has just produced. In the voodoo method the "assassin" would walk right up to the victim, smiling all the way- then "Poof!" After preparing for this moment by taking a lungful of air and tightening your belly to charge, blow the dust off your open hand with a single forceful blast of wind as when blowing out a stubborn candle. Aim for the eyes, intending the particles to elicit the involuntary blinking response of the human eye. This requires only two-hundredths of a second and cannot be stopped without years of practice in staring. Thus, you temporarily blind the opponent and so become invisible. His blindness will last from five to forty-five seconds, depending on the magic powder formula used. In that amount of time, most people can pick up a weapon and beat the enemy senseless, or run away and get help.

SINGLE HAND TOSS

Magicians and illusionists enhance the effect of blinding powders and make them less fearsome by using glitter dust. Symbolically it is the same thing. You "catch the eye" of the audience or attacker and distract them from the real action, enabling the performer to vanish some object or volunteer.

This is the same sparkling, shredded bits of aluminum foil that most children in kindergarten learn to glue onto cardboard, paper and each other. It makes a dazzling display.

These require no preparation after being purchased. The tops of the little plastic tubes come off easily, enabling the user to scatter the spray of metallic color and reflection by simply tossing it upward. Being heavier than dust or ash, the particles will fall more quickly. Therefore the hiding place to which you will flee, having been selected before trying this ploy, must be close at hand.

The Single Hand Toss is the most basic way of delivering the Ninja Dust Bomb, glitter dust, or any similar powder weapon, as well as coins, sand, or a bowl of hot soup. Drop the leading hand, the one nearest the target, to waist level holding the broken eggshell in a loose fist to conceal it from the enemy.

Quickly toss the dust upward, opening your loose fist to spray the powder into the face of the adversary. Again, a little practice goes a long way. You can also toss the dust between you and the adversary to form a temporary screen that will hide you from view long enough to duck away out of sight. Alternatively, toss the eggshell hard up against he ceiling to make him look up at the noise and be showered with dust.

Some ancient wizards added to the confusion of such a display by leaving behind a talisman, magic sign, mouse, frog or bird. The victim of this trick would then unconsciously associate the living creature with the magician and mistakenly assume that the sorcerer had turned himself into the animal. Furthermore, the familiar, pet or beast attracts the attention of the victim, drawing him away from you. This is the basis for the legend that vampires could turn into bats, that illusionists can transform into tigers, and that Ninja could likewise "morph" into some other life form.

The GLITTER MAGICAL WORK

Today the simplest way of applying the old sand-in-the-eye trick is to fill a small plastic bag with flour and loosely seal it with a bit of tape.

The bag can be opened by:

- lifting the flap and dumping the contents through the hole,
- by ripping it in half to create a large display in a single motion,
- or by cutting into the plastic with a finger or thumbnail and tearing a hole through which the powder may be dispersed.

Another method of throwing a handful of sand, dust, or rocks into the face of the enemy is to toss the ruptured bag upward with both hands, as if scooping out water from a bucket.

The method of practicing these techniques is to throw the powder forcefully onto a wall or sheet so that the various splatter patterns can be seen and the most effective throwing method chosen. With a minimal amount of effort even the meek and mild can overcome the high and mighty.

It should be noted that a good deal of attention has been placed on the art of *Shuriken-Jitsu* (throwing stars or darts) with much emphasis on the implements themselves-how many points the have, how sharp they are, how much penetration they achieve, and so on. The masters of the true art, however, will tell you that the real secret of throwing is to be accurate. If the proper method of throwing is learned even a penny can be as deadly as an arrow. One should use the *Tonki* (shuriken) stars, knives or spikes to practice throwing accurately.

Then, anything can be a weapon.

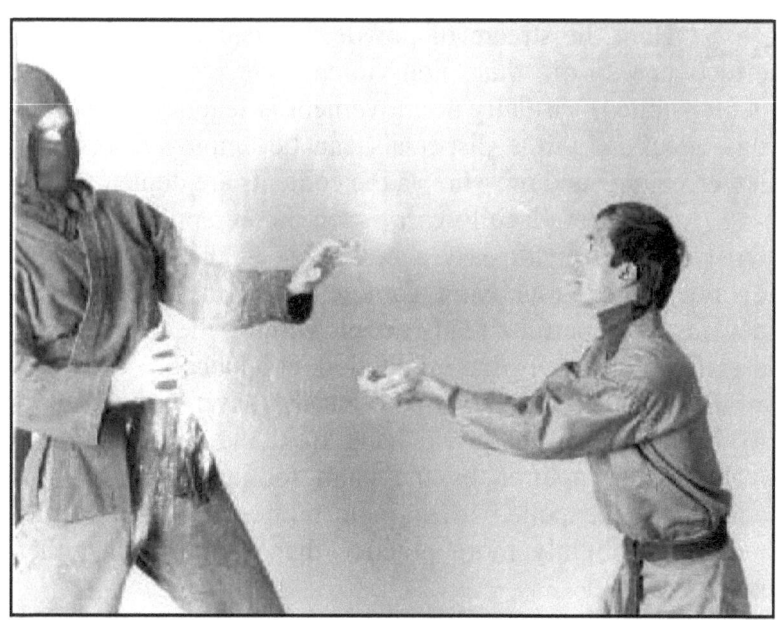

31

SQUEEZE BOTTLE METHOD

Another method of projecting powder into the eyes of an enemy at slightly greater distance is by means of the squeeze bottle. This can be constructed easily by emptying any of the soft plastic containers available on the market today, drying out the inside and refilling it with a finely ground powder, such as talc.

The aperture, or nozzle, must be of sufficient width to permit passage of the particles when pressure is directed against the sides of the container. Furthermore, some sort of loose fitting or easily removed cap must be in place to prevent accidental spillage. Something as simple as a small bit of wax placed over the end can be adequate. The wax will be blown off when the bottle is squeezed.

The Squeeze Bottle, like the Poison Water Gun, increases the effective range of the weapon. It is customary to paint such devices black so they blend into uniform, or flesh tone so they are not easily visible in the hand before use.

Here the stream of powder is clearly seen and the effectiveness of this non-violent weapon is clearly demonstrated. Virtually no movement is required to initiate this attack. Multiple dispersals can be employed, each of lesser volume and pressure as the contents are depleted.

The best place to carry such a contraption is on the wrist or forearm for easy access. One of the reasons why many of the Ninja wore gauntlets was to conceal such devices. This permits ready access without the necessity of delving into pockets that might alert an opponent.

Another alternative is to attach a short string or cord to the bottle so that it can hang from the wrist or waist, ready to be captured by the palm for instant use as the contents are expelled in a single motion. Of course, this requires a slightly more practice than some of the other methods.

KASUMI no JITSU

Suppose, however, that you are caught without your secret weapon? How will you vanish then?

Not to worry- the Ninja have a technique for that unfortunate eventuation of circumstance as well. It is called *Kasumi*, the mist or fog. Given here is the Earth Method for using it.

Stand at Parade rest or Ready Stance, squarely facing the aggressor with hands clasped in back or front and the knees slightly bent. In *Kuji Kiri*, the finger-knitting positions of Ninja meditation, the eighth position is one in which all the fingers are extended wide to symbolize "control of the elements of Nature," a signal to others in the clan of awareness of the Five Elements. In a moment you will signal this, unarmed, to the aggressor in such a way that he cannot mistake the message.

As he steps forward to grab you, deflect his arm by raising both of your arms upward from the shoulder, bending the knees to lower the hips and head defensively and aim the backs of your wrists at his face. Through depth perception, his eyes will see the ends of your arms and judge the danger presented as they come into range. They will seem quite far away, so most people will react slowly to the threat.

Flick the fingertips of both hands upward into his face to make him blink by touching his eyelashes. Again, this elicits an involuntary blink response. Of course, that would be an ideal application. Barring that, any proximity of the fingertips to within two inches of his eyes is sufficient to cause the blink response.

What he would see, if his eyes were open, would be both palms and outstretched fingers in his face; and that would be all. You would thus be hidden behind your open palms, such that he cannot see. You have ducked down and bent your knees.

With your right leg, Cross Step in front and step behind the opponent by pivoting on the right heel, striking him in the chest or throat with your forearm while passing beneath his outstretched arm. This jars his chest and Phrenic nerve in the neck that operates the diaphragm. This injury causes it to slow down so he cannot breathe.

Swing behind him with your left leg and wrap your left arm around his throat to choke him. Hold his head while you press your fist against the base of his skull.

Hold your right bicep in your left hand to form a Figure-4 Lock around his neck. This is a secure hold from Greco-Roman Wrestling. The pressure produces temporary blindness through trauma to the primary cerebral cortex of the brain, which controls all vision. Cut off the blood supply and darkness envelops the victim. After pressure is released, impaired vision will last as long as the pressure was applied to produce the effect.

This is also the position for applying the Japanese Sleeperhold, performed by using your right palm to push the enemy's head forward so that his throat is pressed into the "V" of your left elbow, cutting off the flow of blood to the head by constricting the carotid arteries on both sides of his neck.

When the enemy passes out, you have become invisible.

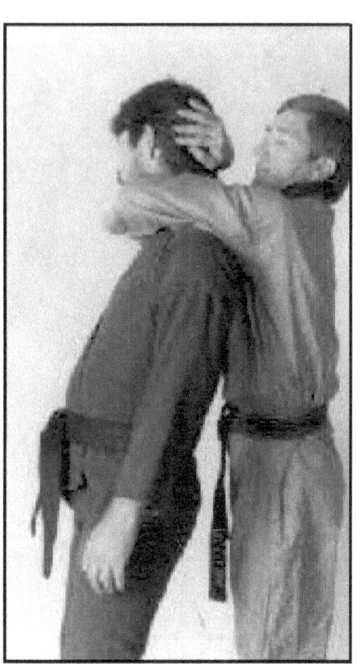

This vanishing technique is the first to be learned because Earth is the first of the Five Elements. It may be used with any of the blinding methods or striking methods given or yet to come. It is a Wood technique that employs spiral action.

There are three types of motion: linear, circular, and spiral. The last being a combination of the first two. Among the Five Elements. Earth is a linear or Yang element as is Fire. Water and Air are circular. The epitome of all techniques- for both linear and circular have their applications- is a combination of the two.

The linear part of the technique is the Hand Flash in the face. Lift straight up, arms and fingers straight. The circular part is the Cross Step behind the opponent. Wood is used to symbolize spiral motion because it represents circular motion around a linear axis, the very pattern of the Universe itself.

It is useful to combine this Kasumi trick from Judo with a loudly shouted command to startle the opponent and make it easier to flick your fingers in his face. In martial arts, this is called a *Kiai*, or spirit shout. It also tightens the belly to stir courage. Development of this technique is a product of meditation and is the test at the end of each book.

SAND-IN-THE-EYES

In many emergency situations a handful of sand may be obtained by suddenly crouching down, as if fearful of being struck, and grabbing a handful in each fist.

1] The Enemy initiates his attack. The Ninja bends his knees and lowers his Center defensively in preparation for the next movement.
2] The Enemy's fist finds no target to strike as the Ninja drops quickly out of sight by bending his knees, both hands fill with sand.

3] As the fist swings past him, the Ninja begins to stand by pushing off strongly with his legs. Both fists are full of sand seized while crouching.

4] Returning to his vertical base, the Ninja throws both hands full of sand into the enemy's face to blind him.

5] Taking advantage of this momentary blindness, the Ninja can easily overcome the enemy or simply vanish to safety.

After very little practice, you can launch the tiny missiles toward the enemy using both hands at once, one hand at a time, or by cupping the hands together. All are equally effective in delivering the weapon and making the enemy look away so you can escape.

BLACK NINJA METHOD

At the time of this writing there is a professional wrestler known as Kendo Nagasaki, the "Black Ninja." The author has often seen him perform. He uses a trick known as the Earth Method Dragon Breath to propel a dry, blinding powder into his opponent's face. At the crucial moment in his bouts, he emits from his mouth a green powdery mist. Opponents struck in the face with this weapon immediately clutch their eyes and writhe on the mat in agony.

While we have no way of knowing for certain if this gentleman performs his feat as it is done in the Koga Ryu system, this is, nonetheless, one such method of dispersing a dry powder from the mouth.

Since bamboo is plentiful in Japan an China, it was only a matter of time before someone got the idea of using a pipe stem to propel darts and powders at the enemy. A small joint of bamboo, filled with powder and capped with wax on both ends, can easily be hidden in the mouth and used as indicated.

The reason it is called Earth Method of the Dragon Breath technique is because dry powder and sand are of the Earth. They are the natural weapons the Ninja is given by the Earth. There are many methods of tossing, throwing, or propelling such missiles. Blowing them out of a tube is properly a function of the Wind (Air), one of the Five Elements. The Dragon Breath Technique is therefore classified as an Air Method. But, one can also spit water, as will be seen in the next section, or dry powder if one but knows how. Some Ninja *ryu* carried tiny blowguns like this with poisoned darts that could be spewed at an enemy if he was foolish enough to try and pull down the Ninja's mask to see his face.

KINDLING THE INNER FIRE

Let's say you have managed to "disappear."
What will you do now?
Well, usually you must hide. That requires patience. So, the Ninja developed the Exercise of Stillness, how to sit and breathe quietly while waiting for pursuit to end. To pass the time, they practiced *Kuji Kiri*, the Japanese version of *Qi Gong* or breathing exercises, to calm the mind and heal the body.

The Body is the vessel that holds the spirit. That is why it represents the Earth Element.

The Breath is the spirit. Many cultures believe that an infant is not alive until it takes its first breath. At that time, it is believed, the spirit enters the body, bringing with it all the knowledge required to exist in an Air environment instead of a water filled one.

The Mind is the will, that binds them together.

Before one can learn to be a "fire-breathing dragon" one must first earn about Fire and Breathing. To accomplish this, the ancients have provided a series of exercises that act both on the conscious and the subconscious levels. They must be learned in the proper sequence given on the fingers, each level building on the one below it. Do not leap ahead, lest injury result.

The fist sep is to draw air into the vessel, then to extract from it the essence required to sustain the body. Just as the digestive system extracts nutrients from food, the lungs extract oxygen from the air.

The Greeks called the vital life-force *pneuma*. The Hindus refer to it as *prana*. The Chinese call it *qi*, the Japanese *ki*. By whatever name, it is not only the molecules of nitrogen, hydrogen, and oxygen that make up our air, but also the electrical potential that holds the atoms together.

When gases change from oxygen to carbon dioxide, a finite amount of energy is released, evident and observable. Accept for a moment the principle of modern physics that energy cannot be destroyed. If so, then the energy released by oxygen being extracted from the air had to "go" somewhere. It is found in the *charkas* or energy wheels of the body, playing on the surface of the skin in the acupuncture meridians and the aura. It is the force of Life. It is exactly this same type of chemical reaction that releases energy to muscles to make fibers contract and the body move. On a molecular level, adenosine diphosphate is transformed into adenosine triphosphate to power the muscles. This is a medical phenomenon known as the Kreb's Cycle.

So, the goal of this first exercise is to extract from the air both the gases needed to maintain life and the *Qi* ("key" or "chee") the Force that is everywhere, filling, penetrating and surrounding all things. In the martial arts this energy is used to harden the body and make it invulnerable to spear, sword, arrow, serpent's fang or tiger's claw.

Any cultivation of the life-force is called meditation.

KUJI KIRI

Sit in the Half Lotus Posture, or Adept's Pose. The right leg is folded beneath the body to sit on the heel. The left leg is folded with the left foot resting on the right thigh. Touching the middle fingertips to the thumbs connects the psychic channels in the arms and prevents energy leaking out of the palms. This is the first of the *mudra*, or finger-knitting positions of *Kuji Kiri*.

Inhale slowly and deeply through the nose, filling the lungs from bottom to top, like pouring water into a glass. This is the first breathing exercise of *Kuji Kiri*. It is called Deep Breathing. Most people only use the upper third of their lungs for respiration.

Draw the air deep into the Tan T'ien, the One Point two inches below the navel, the center of gravity and balance of the physical body, the Golden Stove in Chinese medicine and Ninja Alchemy. This is called "kindling the fire." Note that the lower belly expands as you breathe in and contracts as you breathe out. This is the same lower belly we have said many times should be tightened just as one charges the enemy in combat. Symbolically, the Golden Stove will "cook" the Juice of Jade, described in the Book of Water, until the "steam' rises to the Mysterious Chamber of the head to enlighten the Mind.

Exhale slowly and completely through the mouth by gently compressing the lower belly, expelling all impurities and negative emotions from the body. This is the first relaxation exercise. It is called "sighing," a natural stress-relieving technique instinctively known to all.

The first form to be studied is called Natural Breathing. Most people breathe with their lungs, usually with the upper chest alone. To do so is to limit the amount of lung area available for oxygen exchange. The ancients have taught us to "breathe with the belly." Inhale slowly and deeply letting the lower abdomen, below the belt, expand as if filling with air. This opens the lower lobes of the lungs so more oxygen can permeate the blood. Then let the belly deflate as the exhalation is made. One should repeat this for at least twenty minutes at the beginning and end of each meditation session. For the beginner, however, three or four repetitions are enough to start with lest you hyperventilate.

This exercise will calm the mind, heal the body and improve the digestion. It is sometimes helpful to visualize clean, pure air coming into the body and impurities or negative emotions being gently expelled. Listen to the sound of your respiration and gradually make it slow, soft and silent so it cannot be heard, even by yourself. Then you can hide effectively.

You might want to mentally or verbally repeat some positive affirmation. A short phrase, such as "in comes the good air, out goes the bad air," can be very effective. At the conclusion of each session you will be completely relaxed and refreshed.

What has all this to do with becoming or staying invisible you may ask? Suppose you are confronted by a bully who takes hold of your shirt to prevent your escape and you haven't had time to steal your Black Egg from its secret pocket. Not to worry- you are now armed with Qi, what martial artists call inner strength.

For them, and now for you, Qi is drawn into the Tan T'ien, below the belt, compressed and directed to the fist, forging it into a deadly weapon. Or, it is channeled to some other part of the body to make it impervious to injury or heal a wound. Or, in the case of the Ninja Fire Breathing Dragon Technique, it is used to propel a fireball at a target. This is the first step in developing that technique. It cannot be omitted.

THE USES OF FEAR

When one is frightened, the rate of respiration changes, contributing to and caused by fear. Natural Breathing calms this anxiety and that alone is reason enough to practice it. Now, however, we shall apply it to he art of self-defense.

As fear grows you feel the "bottom drop out of your stomach," because your adrenal glands have been activated by the "flight-or-fight" response; another involuntary reflex common to all human beings. When this happens, take a deep breath. Draw air deep into the belly, filling and expanding it in the same manner as meditating. This will calm the adrenal effect and give you control over your reaction, enabling you to perceive the situation clearly and react spontaneously. Exhale about ten percent and tighten the belly. This helps prevent injury and screws up the courage. The Samurai had a saying, "When afraid, tighten the belly and charge!"

Look the attacker "dead in the eyes" by focusing on his forehead. This is a very subtle trick used by magicians and hypnotists. It makes the subject feel inferior and can be used to intimidate those of lesser will. Fix his attention on your eyes as you inhale. This is a psychological response to his challenge. By engaging his vision you accept and signal to him with your body language that you are preparing to fight. This will make him hesitate. It may even make him release you and give up the battle, preventing further escalation of violence.

If this fails, as you finish inhaling and tightening the lower belly, blow out forcefully into the face of the attacker. Don't try to "blow out all the candles" in one breath and empty yourself. Save some air with which to strike a blow or run away. Even a short blast of air will make him blink and provide an opportunity to escape.

BREATH CONTROL

BLOWING OUT A CANDLE

Here is a practice method for developing this technique. Stand poised in a firm Horse Stance at arm's length from a lit candle. Concentrate on the flame as you breathe in. Without moving closer, practice blowing out the candle by exhaling short puffs of air from the belly. Correct your aim by blowing a steady stream of air and watching for the flame to flicker.

This is a test of *Qi Gong*, breath control. When you can put out the candle with a single puff at arm's length you will have learned the technique. There is no way the enemy can block it or prevent himself from blinking. At that instant, MOVE!

Decide whether to jerk away from his grasp or seize him in a painful wristlock while inhaling, but don't be indecisive-it can be fatal.

Advanced practice for this technique is to put the candle at eye level. Begin by blowing gently until you can see the effects of your breath on the flame. You should be able to make it move back and forth as you inhale and exhale from about three feet away. When you can do that, bend it toward you and away by will alone. Do this for a while, then blow it out in a single puff.

Gradually move farther back until you can snuff it out from about three feet away. Blowing out a candle at eye level is quite different from blowing down onto a table.

Do not strain. Do not sputter. Do not try to go beyond arm's length. The technique can be done from greater distances, but then one tends to whistle or spit unintentionally.

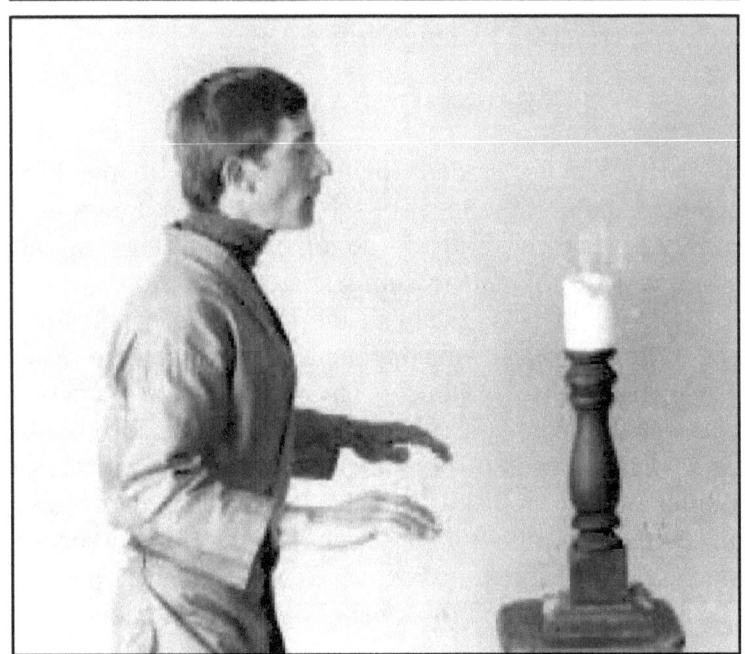

STONE DRAGON FIST

A Shaolin teaching declares, "The Earth Dragon is made of stone. Rooted to the ground it cannot be moved." Stone Dragon techniques include linear punches and kicks, takedowns, breakdowns, and throws to get the enemy on the ground where he can be finished with mat-work techniques. Anatomy, the understanding of the body, the earthy manifestation of the spirit, is learned, just like the vital and fatal points, as demonstrated by the fist-to-the-base-of-the-skull technique, which can also be used to heal. Stone Dragon is only a small part or the Ninja Iron Body system, that enables the user to endure hardship and withstand pain.

The classic Dragon's Head Fist in some styles of Kung Fu is known in Ninjitsu as the Shoulder Punch, in which the fingers are curled into the palm and the thumb folded over to lock them into place. This hardens the fist and exposes the two foremost knuckles of the index and middle fingers as the striking surface.

PUNCHING OUT A CANDLE

The fist is "loaded" palm uppermost on the hip. Place the candle at the level of the solar plexus. Stand in a firm Horse Stance. Extend the other hand edge up as shown, or palm forward to simulate an attempt to ward off an attacker. This is to establish the range that enables the Ninja to find and strike his opponent even in total darkness by using the sense of touch. The target is the Xyphoid Process at the tip of the Sternum. If this is struck with as little as eight pounds of pressure, the diaphragm will cease pumping and the victim will fall to the floor. No permanent injury will result unless he is struck harder. You may never strike an attacker like this, but you do need to develop hand speed and concentration for some of the later techniques.

Throw the punch from the hip, twisting the fist over at the last second to "snap" the punch, stopping just short of the candle flame. The aim is to use air compressed in front of the fist to snuff out the flame without it actually being struck. When you can "punch out" a candle in this manner, you can knock out the average man with one punch. The left arm is snapped back to the left hip as the fist strikes to counter-balance the movement and add to its impact.

Note that this is a linear or straight punch. Compare it to the circular Hidden Fist technique given in the Book of Water. Likewise compare the Edge-of-the-Hand Block with the Lama Hand given in the Book of Wood. This will help you understand the relationship of the Five Elements and demonstrate that they Invisible Fist system is complete and "comes full circle." Because it ends at the same point at which it began.

The Book of WATER

"The Water Dragon resides in the Pool of the Subconscious Mind."

Old Shaolin Teaching

The weapons of the Water Dragon are poison spray like that used in the Ninja Poison Water Gun. This is constructed of two interlocking tubes that, when compressed, act like a large syringe to eject a stream of toxic liquid toward an attacker. There is also the more modern liquid tear gas, as well as self-defense sprays like a water pistol filled with ammonia to drive off dogs or muggers.

Another weapon of the Water category is Breath Control as demonstrated by the ability to remain submerged for long periods of time underwater.

Finally, there is the understanding of the Five Emotions and Five Desires. This is the level of the subconscious mind where a near dream-like state may be induced through auto-suggestion to produce positive long lasting psychological results in a short period of time.

SPIT IN THE EYE

With all the previous discussion about the Tan T'ien and expelling puffs of air from the lungs, one might wonder why not proceed with the next logical step of spitting in the eye of the enemy as a method of temporarily blinding him so you can escape?

This has long been regarded as a heroic if somewhat futile gesture in the face of certain doom. It would seem to be more of an insult or an act of defiance than an attack. It may be that this was how the act was first intended. But, if performed at the right time and followed by one of the Vanishing Steps, it is clearly useful as a means of attaining invisibility.

Spitting, therefore, is an example of a vanishing technique representing the Water Element. Like the previous element Earth, it is known as the Water Method Dragon Breath. Once aware of this technique the wise martial artist is never unarmed. One Kung Fu expert bragged in a recently published martial arts magazine article that he could spit accurately up to ten feet. Accuracy is key. It is not called "in-the-eye" for nothing. The eye is the best target. In fact, it is the only target sufficiently vulnerable to a drop of water to be worthy of mention.

There are various ways to learn this somewhat disgusting technique. Individual experimentation is the best way of discovering the most suitable method. Bear in mind that this is a weapon and not just random rudeness.

Don't aim at the ground. Spitting on someone's boots is an insult and almost certain to elicit a response. But, it is not a "self-defense" move.

Don't "overload" either. Due to the sensitive nature of the eye and the blink reflex, which it will be recalled reacts even to wind, a small amount of water is more than sufficient and easier to generate and propel with any degree of accuracy. When you can project at eye level for about eighteen inches, return to the candle and practice spitting it out. Over time, move the target farther and farther away until you find the natural limit of your range. This should be about arm's length, and represents the limits of one's sphere of influence or "personal space."

As the aggressor prepares to attack, accumulate a mouthful of saliva. Or, if a drink is handy, conceal a sip of the liquid by not swallowing it. Return the stare of the adversary steadily. Being "armed" a defender has a psychological edge and so can act with confidence in the face of danger. Not speaking back against his verbal assault will also confuse him. (Of course, you can't speak because you have a mouthful of liquid.) Thus, the technique produces the body language signals that may, by themselves, forestall his attack.

Before he can launch an assault, however, or at the moment he makes his verbal challenge and demands an answer, spew the liquid into his face and eyes. This will blind him for an instant with no permanent injury. Be sure to be out of sight by the time he wipes his eyes and regains his vision, since this technique will almost certainly infuriate him and his ego, which brought him to this challenge in the first place, will demand revenge.

THE JUICE OF JADE

To demonstrate the degree of detail into which the Ninja delved in order to augment their techniques, we present an exercise known in ancient times as Red Dragon Washes the Waves. It can be done is a seated meditation position, therefore qualifying as an internal exercise, one that circulates the life-force, Qi Gong.

It is, or was, invented by the Chinese as a method of brushing the teeth long before the creation of the toothbrush. Since they recognized that good digestion was largely dependent on proper chewing or mastication of food into nutrients, good dental hygiene became a hallmark of ancient medical practice.

Sitting in a comfortable, cross legged pose with the eyes closed, back straight, and head up, lightly run the tip of your tongue around the inside of your teeth from left to right (clockwise) eighteen times; then from right to left (counter-clockwise) eighteen times. Swish the saliva thus generated back and forth in the mouth thirty-six times and divide it into three portions. Swallow each with a gulp into the lower belly. This exercise stimulates and massages the teeth and gums, removes plaque, and prevents tooth decay. It is also an excellent method of producing spittle with which to practice self-defense. "Brush" twice a day.

The Chinese believe that the saliva is charged with positive and negative ions through the manipulation of the Red Dragon (tongue), which is the reason for the equal number of rotations in each direction.

One should also observe that when the numbers are totaled (18 + 18 + 36) the sum is seventy-two, whose digits add up to nine, the prime number of *Shugendo*, the *Yamabushi* sect of Buddhism associated with Japanese Ninjitsu. In Chinese medicine, nine is a Yang or positive number while six or multiples thereof is considered Yin.

The Chinese call this charged saliva the Juice of Jade and believe it calms the mind, heals the body, and improves the digestion. Certainly, the increase in digestive enzymes alone must produce some beneficial effect. But, beyond this, the three portions swallowed represent Heaven, Earth, and Man, the three levels of being. Thus, a certain degree of philosophy is also included in the teaching. Martial artists know this method as "uniting mind, body, and spirit." Therefore, it is not wise to waste too much of this precious fluid in mere candle extinguishing practice. Just so you will know how to generate such a weapon if need be.

SPEWING WATER

Having accomplished the first exercise, let us turn now to the simplification method. Instead of using personal body fluids to practice spitting, employ a small cup of water and practice spewing small sips and later streams of liquid at the flame. Try to eventually learn to spray the liquid to form the "mist" or "fog" alluded to in the Earth Methods.

Do not sputter, but strive to have the water clear your lips completely using pressure of the lungs and lower belly to expel the smaller amounts in a single jet of spray and the big mouthfuls in a continuous stream. Do not run out of air before you run out of liquid!

From this it can be seen that any liquid could be used in this manner. A cup of coffee becomes a lethal weapon against more than one attacker by spraying a sip onto the leader, throwing the rest at a second enemy so that a quick and unexpected strike can be made to even a third party and an escape effected. Even Chinese tea or hot soup can be thrown like a Ninja Dust Bomb with the same effect. All symbolize the Water Element.

TOBACCO JUICE

Obvious extensions of this technique include the use of tobacco juice. The somewhat disreputable habit of chewing tobacco does have a self-defense function, if one chooses to cultivate it. The reason for bringing it up is more to make one aware of the possibility of such a defense rather than advocate its practice. One of the greatest American cult heroes, Clint Eastwood, used this device in a film *The Outlaw-Josie Wales* (1976) in a classic example of using a "bad" means to achieve a worthwhile goal.

Nicotine poisoning of the eyes will induce great discomfort and temporary blindness. A certain caustic effect should also be anticipated, but is usually not sufficient to cause scarring. Furthermore, the pungent aroma assaults the nostrils of the victim in a manner similar to the Dragon Breath Technique given in the fourth book, Air. It also results in the mental discomfort of being spat upon, stained, and embarrassed.

ACID BREATH

Further discussion of techniques for projecting noxious liquids from the mouth must include some mention of the odd one used by yet another Oriental wrestler of the professional arena, Killer Khan.

He claims to be from Mongolia and performs the salt scattering ceremony of the Sumo ring before each of his matches. Salt can also be used to blind an opponent or rubbed into open wounds to cause discomfort as an Earth technique.

Like the Black Ninja, Khan can, at the critical moment, spew into the face of his hapless opponents a green liquid that stains the face and causes such excruciating pain that they are compelled to clutch their fists to their eyes to relieve it. During this period of incapacity they are invariably pinned by the almost three hundred pound Mongolian.

In Ninjitsu this is known as Acid Breath. It is performed as follows. Hold in the hollow chambers of the mouth until ready for use a chalklike tablet covered in wax to prevent it from dissolving prematurely. When ready, bite into the tablet, filling the mouth with a substance that produces an abundance of saliva as in the Juice of Jade Exercise, only quicker and with less concentration. Simultaneously adding the desired pigment to the mixture. The formula should not be too caustic lest it burn the lining of the mouth and do more harm to the user than the victim. Naturally, the danger of such a trick is accidentally swallowing the mixture or liquid weapon and choking on it. Therefore, do not produce or try to employ too large a quantity of fluid.

An example of this type of article is the frothing blood capsules sold around Halloween to simulate blood from vampire fangs. When chewed or broken open they produce a bright red tint and stimulate saliva production. Food coloring, however, works just as well, as the degree of salivation depends precisely on the amount of saliva required to digest the substance.

A small cellophane pack of water based paint, hidden under the tongue will work as well. When bitten open, the paint, not toxic enough to cause lasting discomfort or poisoning, is distasteful enough to cause profuse salivation. Likewise, if one's bamboo self-contained blinding powder blowgun from the Earth Book were to be accidentally opened it might produce the same effect.

The exact method used by the wrestler in question is unknown, but it must necessarily be based on one or more of these same principles.

It is most certainly of Far Eastern origin and founded on the principles of Chinese medicine, which holds the breath of the liver to be green. Interestingly, the gall bladder in the liver controls the bile, which is green and yellow and bile is the symbol of anger. Bile is stimulated by that emotion. So, without modern scientific methods or having taken the inner journey of meditation, how could the ancients have known these things?

THE ART OF REGURGITATION

Of course, no discussion would be complete without raising the spectre of an even more distasteful and revolting sort of halotoctic attack- projectile vomiting. This technique is born of great mental distress and, without a doubt, life-and-death situations are stressful. Everyone gets "butterflies in their stomach" when nervous; before stepping on stage, for example. This is a manifestation of the reflex required to master the rather obscure and relatively unknown art of voluntary regurgitation.

Harry Houdini is said to have learned this trick from an old Chinese man while working in carnivals and dime museums. He used it to hide his tools and lockpicks from even the most stringent search.

The training method is to tie a small round piece of potato to a string and endeavor to swallow it far enough down the esophagus to make it invisible, then retrieve it by using retro-peristalsis, the reverse muscle contractions that constitute swallowing. If lost, the potato and string will simply be digested. The purpose of the string, of course, is to pull the potato back up the throat the first few times so it won't be swallowed, until you get the knack of regurgitating at will and not from too deeply in the stomach. This technique enables one to overcome the gag reflex in the throat.

The next step is to practice with an egg. When you are confident of being able to conceal and retrieve a boiled or raw egg in practice. Begin using a *Hai Lan*, Black Egg, that holds your secret tools. Again, there is no problem if the practice eggs are lost, they are simply digested, but, don't eat too many at once.

It is also possible to regurgitate spontaneously without prior training merely by being sufficiently terrified. Recruits do it in basic training all the time as a fear reaction to verbal intimidation.

Like many legends about Harry Houdini, this one may or may not be true. But, the method certainly sounds as if it would work and does exist historically. It is yet another example of a technique that trains the Ninja to have conscious control over many autonomic reflexes. One must first control the body, then the mind, then the spirit will soar. As before, one must consider these things in order to understand that there is always a way to achieve a goal, no matter how strange or improbable it may be.

POISON WATER GUN

For the more conservative, other methods include the Ninja Poison Water Gun, counterpart to the Squeeze Bottle in the Book of Earth. It is a device much like a modern syringes. Probably first made of interlocking joints of bamboo with a hole or venturi at the smaller end and closed or sealed at the larger. When filled with marsh water, oil, or similar liquid and pushed together the increased pressure within the tubes propels a spray or stream at or onto an enemy.

In the modern era a favorite weapon of Russian spies was a glass syringe filled with Prussic Acid. When this is discharged into the enemy's face it produces a gas that is instantly fatal leaving virtually no trace other than symptoms of a heart attack. Of course, the agent must dose himself shortly before or after with atropine so as not to succumb to the vapor himself. The weapon is much more easily concealed than a gun.

The famous, or infamous, bank robber Willie Sutton once broke out of prison due in part to his ability to overcome the guards by spraying chlorine into their eyes. He did this by raiding bleach from the laundry room and dispensing it from tennis balls with a slit in one side. Just think what he might have accomplished with a water pistol. Even that simple toy, when filled with ammonia or bleach, can drive off a vicious dog . So, why not a mugger?

HIDDEN FIST

Water, it will be recalled, is a circular element, just as Earth is a linear one. Therefore, it is only logical that a martial art based on these principles should have a representative punch or fist as the others do. We therefore come to the first circular technique of the Ninja Invisible Fist system. It is called the *Mi Chuan*, the "secret hand" or "hidden fist."

When one suffers from anoxia, as caused by the Sleeperhold previously given for example, lack of oxygen to the brain produces disorientation, confusion, and often sparkling spots before the eyes. Many *Judoka* (practitioners of Judo) report that the Japanese Strangle Hold compels the victim to see a "purple haze" just before passing out. This is due to the eye's reaction to the brain shutting down and is one of the last perceptions preceding loss of consciousness.

Earlier we spoke of throwing glitter dust in the face of an attacker to use as a blinding powder. Now we mention the spots before an attacker's eyes just before the purple haze sets in.

From martial arts we now present a method of producing this effect with only one finger, in fact, with only one knuckle.

Fold the fingers into a firm fist but extend the knuckle of the middle finger. Squeeze the other fingers together under it for support. Rap on a tabletop or other wooden surface as if knocking on a door. This hand formation is called the Buffalo Knuckle Fist and is used to "knock" on the enemy's forehead to stun him.

Between and slightly above the eyes is a spot known as the Third Eye. It represents a meeting point for many important nerves and lies directly in front of the central sulci of the frontal lobes of the brain. A sharp blow to this point with the Phoenix Eye Fist, as this technique is also known, will disrupt the flow of nerve impulses from the eyes to the brain- not because great damage has been done, although it is possible for a trained martial artist to fracture to bones of the skull or break them; nor because it injures some psychic center of the brain, even though that is also true. Rather the eyes are impaired because the brain will react to a pain in the forehead, albeit minor, before it will answer signals from the eyes.

Such a blow will make the victim "see spots" before his eyes and may cause them to turn upward or roll up into his head, indicating unconsciousness. A large red spot may appear at the site of the injury and may swell into a lump that can be reduced by applying ice. Almost every time the victim will bring his palm to his forehead, effectively blinding himself by using his own hand to cover his eyes while you escape.

To produce the Purple Haze, strike straight against the Third Eye as opposed to downward as if rapping on a doorway. By traumatizing the nerves, the muscles of the eye relax, dilate, and roll out of focus for three to five minutes.

THE PURPLE HAZE PUNCH

Form the Buffalo Knuckle Fist by extending the middle joint of the middle finger above your fist. Assume the Secret Fist Stance by covering your right isometrically tensed hand weapon with your relaxed open left hand. This prevents the enemy from seeing that you are prepared to strike.

Aim your left shoulder at the opponent to present a smaller target and hide your fist from view. Bend your knees slightly in anticipation of having to duck out of sight quickly and lower your Tan T'ien or center of balance. Look over your left shoulder and fix your opponent's gaze by looking at his Third Eye.

BUFFALO KNUCKLE   HIDDEN FIST STANCE

As the opponent advances intending to seize your uniform or shoulder with his leading hand, take a short step diagonally backward off the line of engagement. In the *Five Element Fist* series, this is the direction of the Water Step.

Lower your head and let him close the distance between you. Sweep his arm aside by swinging your left palm up and outward toward his face in a large circular arc from the previous On Guard Stance. At the same time, swing your right fist out and back in a wide arc to gather momentum for the punch.

The big trick here is the Hand Flash before his eyes to hide the action of your right fist until it is too late to defend against it. This is in keeping with the Ninja tradition of "invisibility first."

Swing the Phoenix Eye Fist in a wide horizontal arc to strike the opponent on the left temple. This is a stunning blow, much more likely to produce unconsciousness or swelling, black eyes and even broken bones, since the bones of the temporal region are much thinner than those of the forehead. It produces shocking pain in the head and numbing blindness for many minutes. But, it is presented here because you may someday need to knock out an attacker who cannot be stopped any other way.

This wild right hook punch is called a "haymaker" in Western boxing, and is therefore a valid technique. It comes over the leading shoulder of the opponent and has a lot of impact when the shoulders and hips are turned into the swing to add momentum. Not only will the opponent "see spots," he will be knocked out with one punch.

1] Sweep his arm aside with the Hand Flash

2] Swing the right fist in a wide arc to strike his head while he can't see the punch coming

3] Escape while he is stunned and seeing spots

[rear view]

Hand Flash before his eyes   Strike over his arm

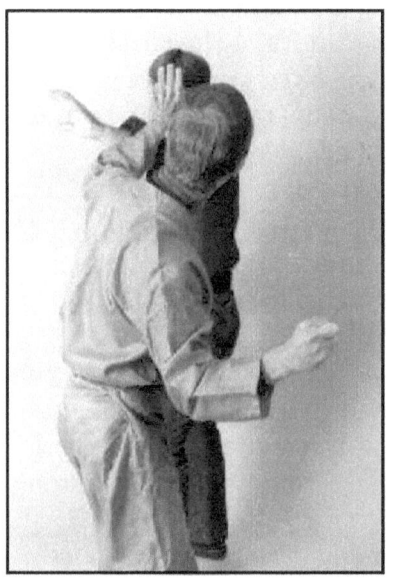 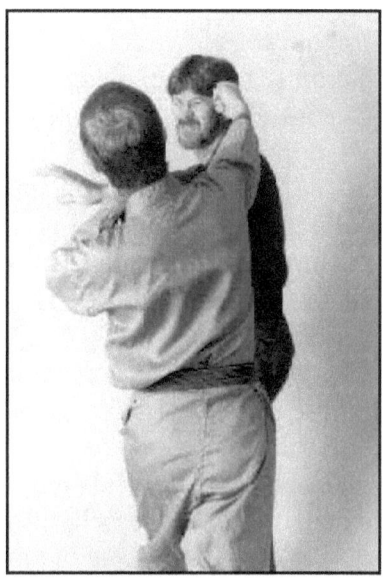

    If executing the "knocking" technique let the fist swing up and over to strike down on his forehead. In the knocking on the forehead method, the fist makes a circle upward, across the chest, above the eyes and down onto the forehead after the Hand Flash is executed. Both are circular motions representative of the enveloping nature of Water.

    This *Mi Chuan* technique is the first technique of the Invisible Fist Sea Dragon (Water) Method. It can be learned quickly and easily by anyone and is almost instinctive when trying to fend off an attacker. For this reason a large number of people can be trained in its use in a short period of time. Making it possible for the Ninja to "raise an army" virtually overnight.

HARAKI

There is a branch of martial arts known and studied by only a few called *Harak*i. It is a Japanese word, composed of the ideograms for *Hara* or Tan T'ien, the center of gravity of the physical body and *Ki*, their term for Qi, previously discussed and defined.

Haraki involves training oneself to draw in air, collect it and cultivate it in the center (inhaling breath), then transmit it with a shout, known in Karate as a *Kiai* or spirit-shout (exhaling breath). The effect is to tighten the belly so you can charge.

It is a cry, a scream, a yell of total commitment. Not at all like the mere grunts of so many other martial arts schools. The warrior puts all his strength and energy into one powerful finishing or deciding blow. It is a strong exhalation from the belly just as a strike is delivered.

It is often seen and properly performed in *Tamieshi-wara*, or breaking demonstrations. Here the students shatter boards or bricks with their bare hands. As indicated in the Book of Earth, such a shout can be included in the execution of various vanishing or misdirection techniques.

In the martial arts, military training, and law enforcement, the value of a deep commanding voice is well recognized and documented. Just as the hypnotic voice will be important to the material covered in the Book of Air. Many a dispute has been settled by a firm tone and a steady timbre, and verbal orders in the field that drive young men into direct gunfire are the result of a programmed response initiated in basic training.

The relationship of this to water is that sound waves can be seen on water, making an invisible phenomenon visible. Thus, the Water element is associated with sound and sound waves.

The effectiveness in combat of the *Kiai* is well documented. It can "freeze" an opponent in mid-step, startle him enough to make him jump out of his stance, or make him blink. The *Kiai* is all that is required.

The range of the *Kiai* is somewhat more extended that the Blow-In-The-Face technique, since the operating factor is sound rather than mere air. Some schools believe that all things are merely vibrating at different speeds. Solids are the slowest, then liquids, then air, fire, and finally wood. Within these are the vibrational planes of light and sound, each of which has a range above and below that which is perceptible to humans. Infrared rays are too long to be visible to the human eye. But, are so active that they break down chemical bonds. There exists sounds that are too low of a wavelength to be heard but that can be felt on the skin, and whistles of so high a pitch that only dogs can hear them.

Thus, sound is also a force that can be used as a weapon to temporarily blind an opponent.

REVERSE BREATHING

The meditation practice for *Haraki* is known as Reverse Breathing. To perform this, let the belly contract as you inhale and expand as you exhale, the reverse of Natural Breathing. This is the mechanism whereby Qi is refined in the lower belly. It is essential that both of these methods of breath control be practiced and learned well.

Again perform about twenty minutes of this exercise in a relaxed and gentle manner. If one considers that Natural Breathing is a way of drawing in positive energy or Qi from the air then it must follow that this energy is eventually transported to other parts of the body. This circulation occurs naturally without conscious direction, otherwise life would cease to exist. With this practice, however, we begin to take conscious control of such autonomic reflexes so that mental direction of energy is also possible.

In a purely hydraulic way, such manipulations of the mental state will produce unconscious tension in certain parts of the body and this will pump or shunt blood to other parts. In Yoga, sitting in the Full Lotus Pose soon puts the legs to sleep by restricting circulation, at least in the early stages. In so doing, the blood is allowed to collect at the base of the spine. By tensing the belly, this excess can be pumped to the brain, symbolically "letting the steam rise" in Qi Gong. When coupled with the nervous impulses that must necessarily accompany such an event, and mental imagery that reinforces the process, one can stimulate the powers of the mind. Or, so it is said.

Even modern science admits that man uses only a small portion of his available brain cells and that a method of stimulating brain activity would be of benefit to mankind. By "charging up" the Qi from the air through hyperventilation in the first exercise one has also oxygenated the bloodstream.

In the Full Lotus Pose a certain amount of this blood has accumulated at the base of the spine, ready for the Sacral Pump, pulling in on the lower belly in rhythm with the heartbeat, to push this oxygen rich blood to the brain.

In Reverse Breathing, this blood floods over the brain, enriching and stimulating the entire organ. Unlike other parts of the body, the brain does not have an extensive network of capillaries to supply blood. Instead, it is essentially bathed in cerebro-spinal fluid while floating in the shallow brainpan of the skull. So, the effect for the user is often like "lighting up the sky" or as in the Zen texts, "opening of the thousand petal lotus." A symbol for the cortical surface of the brain.

Of course, such transcendental experiences cannot be adequately described in mere words, otherwise they would not be transcendental. Suffice to say, it is a unique experience what will make you feel better, think clearer, and be more alert, although completely and relaxed ready to meet whatever the day may bring.

THE HEAVENLY POOL

Now that the inner fire has been kindled with Natural Breathing and the Qi refined by Reverse Breathing in the Golden Stove and the distillation of this raised to the Mysterious Chamber by way of the Heavenly Pillar of the spine all that remains is to let it condense and return to the Tan T'ien to complete the Small Heavenly Cycle of Qi and begin the process of insuring peace of mind, good health, and longevity.

This is accomplished by touching the tip of the tongue to the roof of the mouth. The palate, tongue, teeth and so on are known as the Heavenly Pool in Chinese medicine, where the Juice of Jade originated that was boiled to make the distilled vapor above. What is important, however, is that this chamber forms a gap in the energy channels of the body only bridged by this exercise to let the Qi flow freely.

SHOUTING OUT A CANDLE

Practice "shouting out a candle" by assuming a Horse Stance at arm's length from the target. Inhale slowly and deeply, filling the lungs from bottom to top.

Exhale forcibly, from the belly shouting a one syllable command word, using the diaphragm to direct the sound at the flame. Tighten the belly as you shout.

Virtually any explosive sound can be used for this *Kiai*. "Ha!" "Fish!" Even "KIAI!" itself. Or, a recognizable word such as "Stop!" "No!" or "Wait!" can be employed.

All of these words or syllables are "plosive" in that they expel air from the lungs to produce the sound. The sound used in meditation "Om…" on the other hand is made by closing the mouth and humming, this has a calming effect, which is why it is used for meditation rather than combat.

SILENT *KIAI*

Practice *Haraki* by assuming a firm Horse Stance at arm's length from the candle. Clench the fists around the thumbs and set them on the hips. Concentrate the Qi and focus on the candle.

Without moving, exhale forcefully from the belly making NO SOUND. Direct the exhalation at the flame and extinguish it as before. This time using the "silent *Kiai*."

Compare the posture and facial expression in this technique and the previous exercise. It will be seen that in the former, chest compression expels the air and sound, while the second uses a forceful compression of the belly to direct silent sound waves toward the target.

The GREAT TAI CHI SYMBOL

This is used by many Tai Chi Chuan Schools as a representation of the primordial nature of the their martial art. Its meaning is taken to imply the Grand Ultimate Fist system of health and self defense.

Overlay this symbol on top of the Five Elements chart to demonstrate that Earth and Fire are Yang, on the right side of the symbol while Air and Water are on the left, Yin, side. Thus illustrating the synchronicity and hidden meaning of these symbols. Yang from the sun descends to the center of the Earth where it reverses polarity and rises as Yin energy, returning to the sun to reverse polarity and again become Yang. And so on, *ad infinitum.*

The Book of FIRE

"Time is the fire in which we burn. The Fire Dragon lives in the flame..."

Surit Khan- Thuggee Grandmaster

Given here for the first time ever in print anywhere is the secret method of Eating and Breathing Fire. Both must be learned, or neither, for they are the penultimate Yin and Yang of Qi Gong Exercises of this Way. There is no better or more terrifying weapon.

Thusfar we have discussed two of the Five Elements, Earth and Water. Represented symbolically by the pinky and ring fingers. The middle finger of the hand represents the Fire Element. Within this digit flows the Heart Governor Meridian of Acupuncture and the Yang Yu psychic channel of the arm terminates at the tip of this finger. As well as many major nerves of the arm.

In this section we shall present the physical representation of the Fire Element as taught to members of the DOJO-Academy of Martial Arts who train in Black Dragon Ninjitsu. This Art has been described in many ways. As "savage and terrifying" as the "dark side" of the martial arts, and other misnomers. All part of the Ninja technique of *Monami no Jitsu*, translated to mean, "a head dress seen from four sides looks the same." In other words, a great deal of the world's misery is caused by fear and misperception.

Sometimes the Ninja deliberately confuse the issue. An example of the sort of secret encoding found in modern martial arts is the Tai Chi Symbol seen at the beginning of this chapter. There are many methods of presenting this oft seen Yin-Yang/Tai Chi Symbol.

Usually it is given as a circle, divided by an S-shaped line, black on one side white on the other each side containing a spot or seed of the other.

But, there is only one proper presentation of this primordial symbol so that its meaning is clear. Naturally it is the most ancient and basic.

The original meaning of this symbol was that Yang energy came from above, the Sun or Heaven, and descended to the magnetic center of the Earth where it reversed polarity and rose as Yin energy back toward the Sun, and reversed its own polarity to repeat the cycle.

Thus the circle should be divided by a backwards "S" to symbolize the clockwise direction of time, with the white (Yang) on the right side beginning at the top and being full at the bottom holding a spot of Yin to represent the reversal of polarity and black on the left (Yin) rising toward the spot of Yang above it.

Any other representation is coded because no others have an explanation like this. So, it is not only the Ninja who have their secrets.

There is no other book that teaches Fire Breathing Technique. It is a magician's secret hitherto transmitted verbally only from Sorcerer to Apprentice.

IT IS REVEALED HERE FOR THE FIRST TIME EVER IN PRINT! It belongs with other "torture tricks" like walking on burning coals or piercing the cheek with needles. All of which rely for their efficacy on some subtle physical principle. Although they may seem fantastic and incredible, most are relatively simple and require primarily the will to carry them out.

As the popular magician Penn Gillette once remarked when about to perform this stunt, "One should ask not so much HOW this is done, but rather WHY anyone would want to do it in the first place." The reason is as complicated as the study of invisibility itself; which is to say it is simple.

Basically such performances are a public display of Power, mystical or otherwise, intended as much to impress the audience as it is to develop still greater mental control of the autonomic nervous system. And this, is yet another form of self-discipline. It takes steely nerves and a steady hand to do the Fire Eating Trick. Still, it is but another small step on the path.

There is no trick to Eating Fire. It is a matter of concentration and understanding the nature of the flame. Sideshows and sorcerers have demonstrated this ability through the ages as a method of showing their skills. It is a question of passing one's own test by performing in public as well.

Symbolically, such a performance gives the impression that the wizard or Ninja nourishes himself on elements beyond the comprehension of mere mortals. This then is transmuted into magical powers, like making the user impervious to injury by fire. The presentation may include other feats of strength or walking on broken glass, but the rationale in the mind of the observer is always that the magician has the ability to ingest and absorb the power of the ancient mystical Fire.

So, what is the performer saying with this demonstration?

Some say that he is simply demonstrating the Secret of Life; albeit in a dramatic fashion. For whatsoever a man or mind may cultivate or imitate, so must he become. The cycles of respiration, digestion and circulation shown by any of the ancient sciences is not only essential for life to exist, but the same laws and principles apply on every level.

Must not a man breathe? Drawing in Air, cultivating it by the exchange of gases in the lungs, circulating it to the body to sustain life and expelling with it all negative thoughts and emotions. And if a man breathes fresh air or breathes in a particularly efficient manner is it not better for the working of the body? And, if he stops breathing will he not die in a few moments?

Is it not necessary for a man to drink? Swallowing water from which fluids are produced. Have not even modern sciences told us that 90% of the body is water? The rest being a small handful of chemicals. Isn't it absorbed and changed into and through tissue and expelled having ended its journey through the body by passing through the filtration of the kidneys, carrying away impurities. If we stop drinking, don't we die in a few days?

Isn't Earth itself also represented? In the form and variety of food. And, isn't the pattern the same? As one anatomy professor described it, "The body is essentially a tube within a tube; put something in one end, something comes out the other." Digestion is more complicated than water absorption in terms of the number of organs devoted to it, but the pattern is the same. Bear in mind that life can only exist within a certain acid-alkaline pH range of the blood. This is determined by the rate of respiration and the quality of the air. Likewise, too much fluid, congestion of the lungs for example, can be fatal; just as can dehydration.

So, an equilibrium must be established here as well.

That is why the ancients and now modern man placed such emphasis on proper diet. If you eat "junk food" it is mostly sugar. The body loves this. All nutrients are eventually converted to glucose, a type of simple sugar, for use by the muscles. Such foods are easy to digest and take into the system. But, in time the lack of fiber causes the intestines to suffer and one may develop a malabsorption syndrome so that essential minerals and vitamins cannot be obtained. In this way an imbalance is created that leads to illness and disease.

That is the nature of medicine, to relieve suffering and restore the balance. One must take great care in tampering with the balance. One method is by regulation of diet. Do not diabetics monitor their blood sugar level and supplement or disperse as needed? They also regulate this level by exercising or taking insulin.

That is the nature of this teaching.

Chinese medicine says that one must do nothing to excess. Observing moderation in all things. And, that circulation is the key to good health and longevity. They have devised many methods and techniques. The ones presented here are but one series. Nonetheless, they lead to an understanding of the order of things.

So, we must have water and air, and if we stop eating to we not die in a few weeks?

Why then should it not be the same with fire?

That is why the audience attributes magical power to the magician. Because they recognize this pattern of the Five Elements on an intuitive and subconscious level. That is WHY the magician learns to eat fire. Because he knows the pattern holds true for all elements. Demonstrating this ability to others confers upon him the mystic power of Charisma. First, by teaching him to do something that very few others would even attempt. And, secondly by giving him confidence gained through knowledge and practice.

THE SUBTLE BREATH

In order to perform Fire Breathing Dragon one must develop sufficient breath control to emit a steady stream of air for a long period. This air will form a column around the flame to be manipulated and protect the tissues of the mouth and lips.

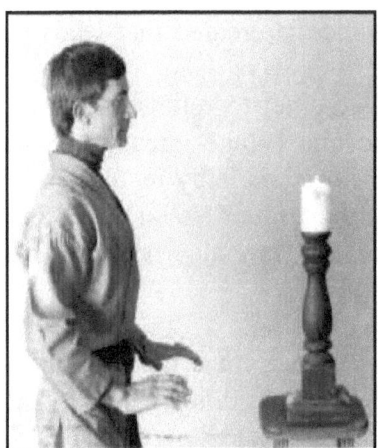 

Stand facing the candle at arm's length in a Horse Stance with your hands relaxed and your mouth slightly open. Inhale deeply, filling the lungs from bottom to top.

Tighten the lower belly and project the Qi at the flame by steadily compressing the abdomen. Send out a steady stream of air that can be directed at the flame.

Because of the slow and steady nature of this column of air rather than a forceful or sharp movement this technique is sometimes considered to be a subtle use of the life-force itself, the Qi (physio-electro-chemical energy) that activates and stimulates the nerves of the body. Hence, it's classification with the Fire Element.

The idea here is not so much to "snuff out the candle" as it is to make the flame bend away from your breath until almost the end of the exhalation, then finish off with a final sharp push. Remember always to retain 10% in the body so you don't have to gasp for air when done.

The abdomen should be taut and most of the air forced out of the lungs by dynamic tension. In the same way, learning how to expel a ball of air from the abdomen makes it possible to snuff out a candle from a much greater distance than by blowing on it. And, prepares the user to expel his breath in such a way that it can be used to control the flaming torch used for Fire Breathing and Eating. This Subtle Breath can also be projected along tabletops to move small objects without physical contact.

FIRE EATING

The technique of eating fire is performed as follows:

First, construct three small torches by wiring cotton swabbing to a metal rod. It should be about ten inches long and the tip should be about one and one-half inches long.

Second, place a small jar of gasoline in a bowl of sand to serve as fuel. Third, have a damp washcloth or towel handy and a sheet of tinfoil in which to put out the torches by smothering.

A lighter or match is used to ignite the torches, which should be seared and packed several times to burn off any threads that might turn into embers. Also, it is best to light one torch then extinguish the match. A candle on the table is a distraction and another fire hazard to worry about.

NEVER BRING A LIT TORCH NEAR THE FUEL!

In fact, once the torch has been lit at the start of the performance, it is unlikely that it will need to be re-soaked or saturated with any further gas during the entire demonstration. The impressiveness of using real gasoline, taking torches out of the jar and always holding the padded end downward so gas doesn't "run up the arm," throwing some of the excess on the ground where it can be identified by the pungent smell, then lighting up, is a spectacular opening.

A word of caution should be said regarding the fuel. Only use WHITE GAS. Red gas is treated with a dye to differentiate it and contains lead that will cause heavy metal poisoning similar to ingesting mercury over a period of time. This can be fatal.

Also gas fumes can be inhaled and cause eye damage or attacks of sinusitis. Swallowing gasoline, or holding it in your mouth is harmful to the teeth and gum, since vapors and hydrocarbons are absorbed directly into the sensitive tissues.

There is also a good deal of soot to contend with. It smokes and dehydrates the roof of the mouth and blackens the teeth. Not to mention a certain amount being breathed in by the nostrils. It does, however, make an impressive flame. It is the fumes that actually burn, not the liquid gas itself.

The heat from putting the torch, which may appear small when not lit but makes a long trailing flame, is not intense or even uncomfortable. Although to the onlooker it seems so. It is sufficient, however, to dry out the tissues of the mouth, the Heavenly Pool.

Alcohol and other fuels burn much hotter than gasoline. The reason gas is such a powerful fuel in cars is because the burn rate is rapid and the mist of the fumes is compressed by the cylinder before the spark ignites it.

Some have found success with lighter fluid, not the new Butane type, rather the older petroleum distillate that was absorbed by the wick of the lighter.

But, again, the effects of the compound on skin are somewhat severe.

Ancient Ninjitsu texts speak of using strong wine as fuel. Certainly they were aware of the fermentation process and capable of distilling a potent alcohol brew suitable for internal consumption for those so inclined. Yet, flammable enough to perform the magic feat.

One trick, known as the Flaming Finger, consists of dipping a digit into strong spirits and passing it through a flame to catch fire. So long as the finger is kept moving the flame may dance on the skin without harm to the user.

This is because the effect of the movement conducts heat away from the flame, making it cool enough to endure without injury. This makes a good warm-up trick.

The secret of Fire Eating is blowing on the flame. Not in any way so an onlooker can detect it. Nor, considering the biological effects, should it be considered "cheating." It is simply the further application of the same Flaming Finger Principle.

After all, is not heat what we want from the fire? And, isn't it absorbed by the proximity of the torch to the body?

Isn't it so that the Chinese have used such treatments as *Moxibustion*, the placing of small cones of *mugwort* over certain acupuncture points and slowly letting them burn down to stimulate the flow of energy for centuries? In this case, we are stimulating the Pineal Gland in the center of the brain by warming the palate.

So let no one say that Eating Fire is a sham. If it is, let them come up and try it. It takes long practice and great determination, but it can be done. The question is whether it is worth the effort is left up to the individual. We believe that to know how is sufficient.

EATING FIRE

Practice first with an unlit torch to develop the confidence, skill and technique required to perform this feat of derring do. Also, some students find that they try to go "too deep" when practicing activating the Gag Reflex in the throat.

It is a good idea to put a bit of Vaseline Petroleum Jelly around the lips. This is to prevent accidental injury and drying of the mouth. One need not be clean shaven for this trick. If done carefully the flame will not singe the moustache or beard.

Tilt the head well back so that you can look at the sky. Holding the unlit torch in the right hand, bring it overhead and slowly down into the mouth.

This slowness is for dramatic effect and so you can control the intensity of the flame by breathing on it. Having learned the inhaling and exhaling breaths in the previous sections, draw a large quantity of air into the Tan T'ien and compress it with the diaphragm as the torch is lifted. Hold the torch at an angle such that if it were lit the flame could rise vertically without burning the fingers. As the torch nears the face, open the mouth wide and exhale slowly from the belly in a steady stream of air. It is sometimes helpful to say the syllable "Haaaa..." when breathing out in this manner. In Chinese medicine, this is the sound of the heart, an organ associated with the Fire Element.

The exhaled air, performed exactly as if doing the *Kiai* Exercise or Shouting Out A Candle, only slower, must form a column of air around the flame and blow it back toward the handle without extinguishing it. In so doing, it cools the flame and prevents injury due to heat.

Do not "run out of air' before withdrawing the torch. If you do, when it is lit, you will suck the flame down your throat and be burned. That is why there is so much emphasis on breath control.

Neither let the torch touch the sides of the mouth, since, even though moist tissues, they can be burned. Touching the roof of the mouth or the tongue elicits a response that closes the mouth. This instinctive reaction smothers the flame immediately. But the lips may be burned by the hot metal handle of the torch. Also, one may gag if this occurs. Other than that, the danger is very slight.

One Snuffs the Torch by quickly closing the lips, not the teeth, around the handle as if clapping the hands. This smothers the flame. Open the mouth and withdraw the torch. Swallow dramatically and the illusion is complete.

After much practice with an unlit torch, visualize the flame on the tip and imagine the heat. Pretend the fire is there. This adds to the positive mental imagery of the practice since no injury can occur. But, the user will learn safety by imagining the torch to be lit.

IGNITING THE TORCH

A] Hold the torch in the right hand and the lighter or match in the left so that the audience can clearly see them.

B] Ignite the torch, making an impressive display of the flame and set the lighter down.

C] Let the flame flare by holding the torch vertically for dramatic effect

TASTING THE FLAME

A) Slowly and dramatically lower the torch toward your lips. Open the mouth wide and begin blowing a gentle column of air towards the flame, "pushing it" back from the tip. Note the angle of the torch.

B] Continue to lower the torch, blowing the flame away from the lips.

C) Let the torch pass the lips while maintaining a steady stream of air pressure around the flame

D) Continue blowing the column of air back as you withdraw the torch. For dramatic effect, lick the lips and wipe them with the fingers as if "tasting" the flame or as a simulation of heat and danger.

E) Pause dramatically, letting the flame flare again, creating the illusion that all of the flame except the small part visible above the lips was inside the mouth

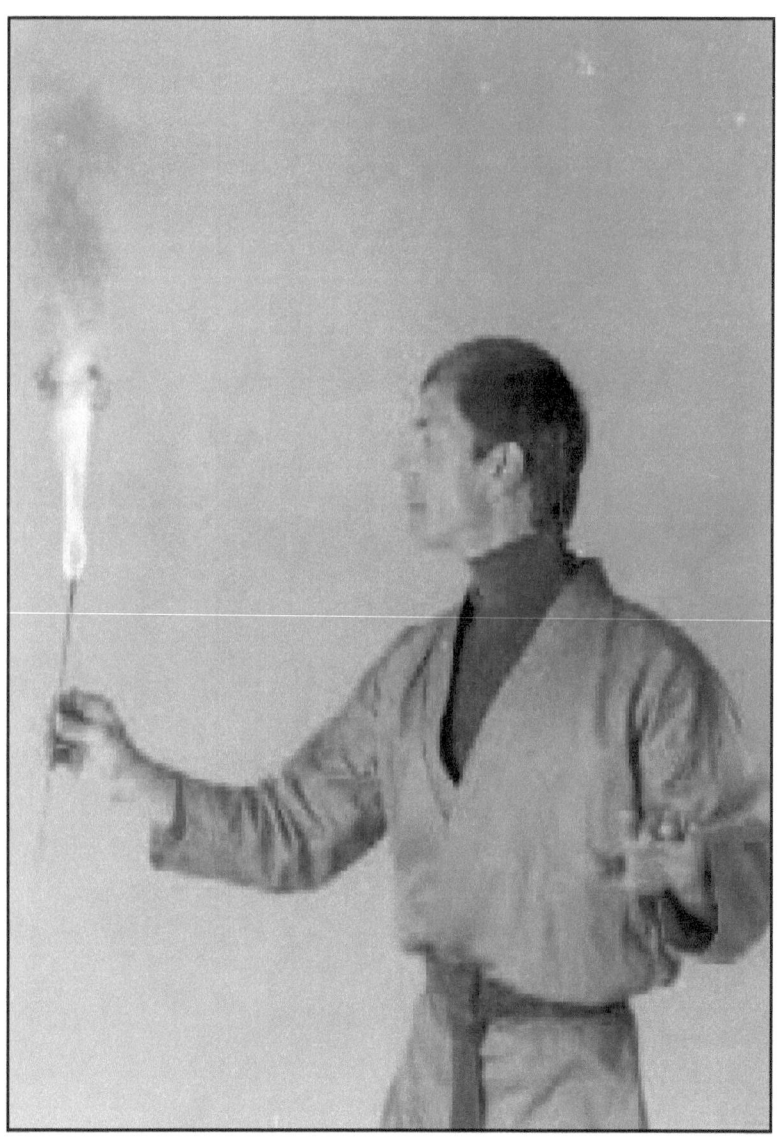

FIRE EATING

A) Lower the torch again toward the lips, blowing on the flame as before Place the tip of the torch inside the mouth, holding the flames back with the column of air. Then close your lips quickly to snuff out the torch.

B) This only takes a second. Holding the mouth closed may cause burns to the lips from the heat of the metal handle. Open the mouth and withdraw the extinguished torch. Swallow dramatically, creating the illusion ha the flame has been "eaten."

When fully confident one may wish to attempt this stunt. Trusted companions should be on hand to witness the experiment and render any First Aid that many be needed.

Don't overdo it. Once successful, many initiates practice incessantly. Like anything else done to excess, this can be injurious. Re-read the section on the effects of Fire in the mouth and use a little prudence.

A final note on the torches. When finished, smother them out by placing the tip on a sheet of tin foil and twisting to diminish the flame, then fold the foil over the torch to extinguish them and safely prepare them for storage. The torch, when in use, should not be soaked with fuel. Barely damp is more than enough. As indicated, slinging off the excess until no drops appear usually provides the proper saturation amount.

LAZY FIRE EATING

For the timid we offer the Lazy Fire Eating Trick. It is performed in exactly the same manner as the former, except it is done with the lighted end of a chopstick or a long fireplace match. Bear in mind that wood burns hotter than gasoline.

Perform as previously described, tilting the head, lowering the torch at an angle that permits the flame to be controlled by the column of air. Once inside the Heavenly Pool, quickly close and open the lips on the unlit "handle" above the flame to smother it out. You must be quicker to put out the flame. Also, a certain amount of ash is inevitable.

In the case of the Fireplace Match, the tip, made of phosphorus, may glow and become an ember that can fall off in the mouth and burn the tongue. But, even a wooden chopstick is prone to burn rather quickly and drop a bit of charcoal on the tongue.

The same care must be exercised when doing this stunt as in legitimate Fire Eating. There is no place in magic for carelessness. Not only does it make for a lack luster show, but often is downright dangerous for the performer. Keep in mind that heat rises. This is the reason for tilting the head back, so the throat is almost vertical. Do not be surprised if you develop a sore throat or even if the tonsils swell up when beginning this practice. This is the body's reaction to greater than normal heat. Just like when you have a fever.

FIRE BREATHING DRAGON

We now present the technique known as Fire Breathing Dragon. Certainly the most spectacular demonstration of the Fire Principle and the exclusive symbol of the Black Dragon School.

We have shown how the system conforms to the myths, legends and realities of dragon lore. From the gaseous attacks of the Air Element to the mist methods of Water and the powders of Earth, the evolution of this magic has been explained in simple and concrete terms.

What better example of the mystic lore than the Fire Breathing Dragon?

This single technique is responsible for the fantastic reputation as fighters enjoyed by the members of the *Hai Lung Ryu* (Black Dragon School).

For what could be more terrifying than knowing that any second you could be engulfed in a ball of fire at the command of the Ninja? This, and other techniques contained herein, are the basis for the claims of "no physical contact" being necessary to overcome an opponent made by some schools of Kung Fu in the early days.

It is not rare, even in this day and age, to see men performing the Human Flame Thrower Technique. A few years ago the streets of Brazil and Haiti were filled with them. They would dash along the vehicular traffic and perform for a dollar. So don't get the idea it is some ultra secret art that can never be told or understood or discovered by others.

These individuals may have been using white gas or 100 proof alcohol known as Everclear, used in the manufacture of wine coolers. Even the aforementioned lighter fluid. But, the method is always the same.

Taking a swallow of fuel the performer would spew out the contents across the top of an open flame like a small torch or lighter. Whereupon it would be ignited and blown into a huge ball of fire. Naturally, this lasted only a moment, but it was impressive nonetheless.

Some of the performers would squeeze their cheeks between thumb and middle finger to gain extra distance and pressure and to make sure all the fuel cleared their lips on the exhalation.

This is the danger.

Should the performer fail to expel all the fuel completely, he runs the risk of having the flame "back-up" the stream of liquid and set himself on fire.

THIS IS NOT A GAME!

IT IS DANGEROUS IN THE EXTREME!

BE CAREFUL!

[Neither the Author nor the Publishers assume any responsibility nor liability for the use or misuse of any techniques presented in this text. The techniques are presented solely as a historical analysis of an ancient and mysterious martial art.]

A) Holding the lit torch in the left hand and a small glass of petrol in the right.

B) Keep an eye on the flame as you take a small sip of the white gas. DO NOT SWALLOW!

C) Set the glass aside and put the thumb and middle fingers on the cheeks to help expel the fluid and wipe the lips if need be.

106

D) Look at the top of the flame and aim your spray or mist so that it passes over the flame to be ignited. Spitting onto the torch, even with gas, would smother the flame.

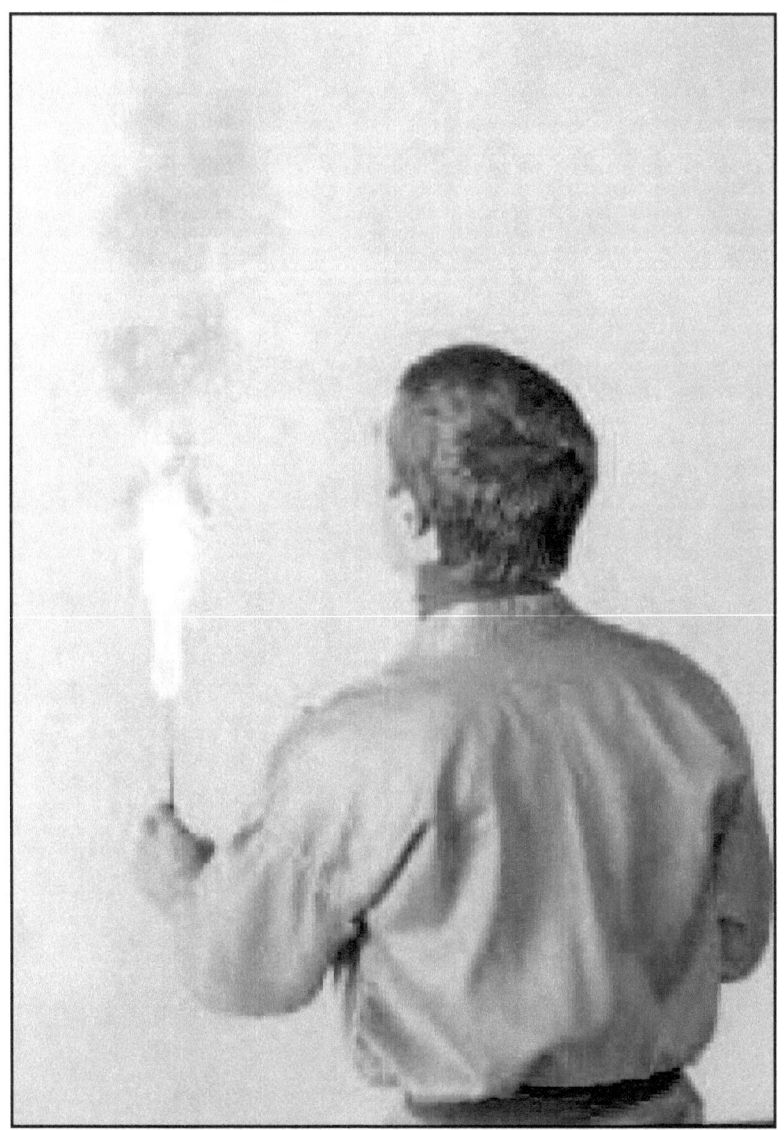

E) Spray a strong, short burst of petrol over the top of the flame to create the fireball.

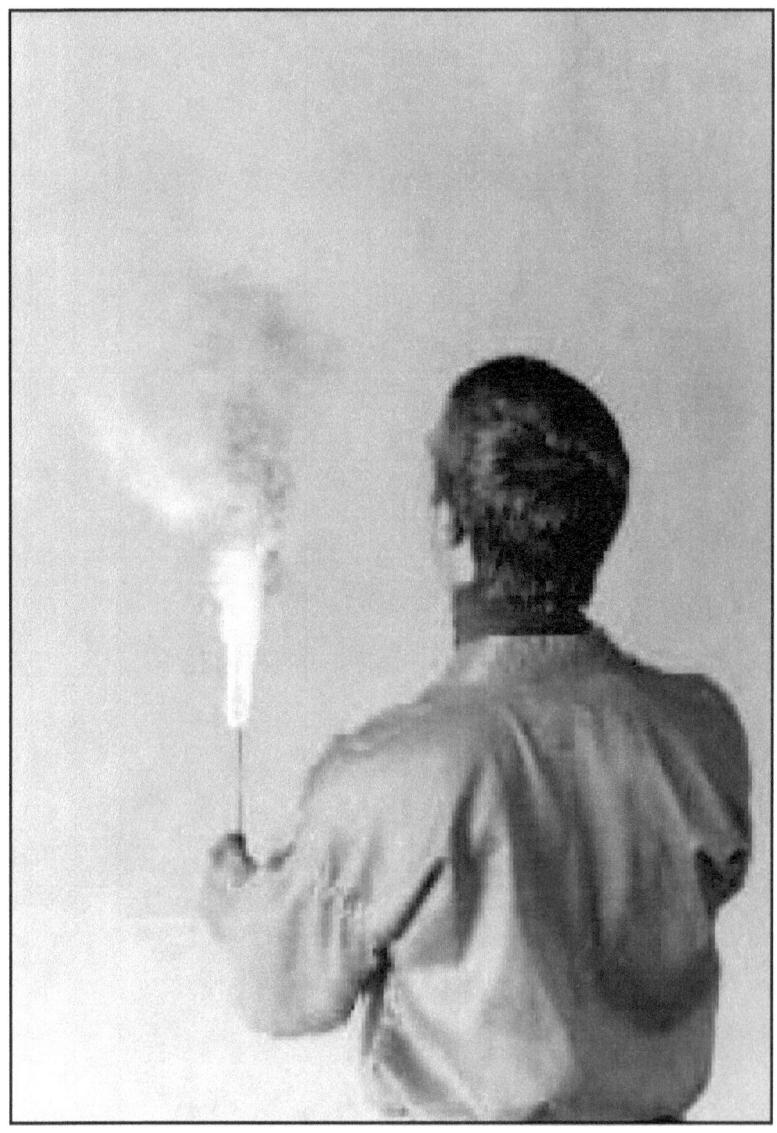

HUMAN FLAME THROWER
[Fire Breathing Dragon-Side View]

A) Holding the lit torch in the left hand and a small glass of petrol in the right.

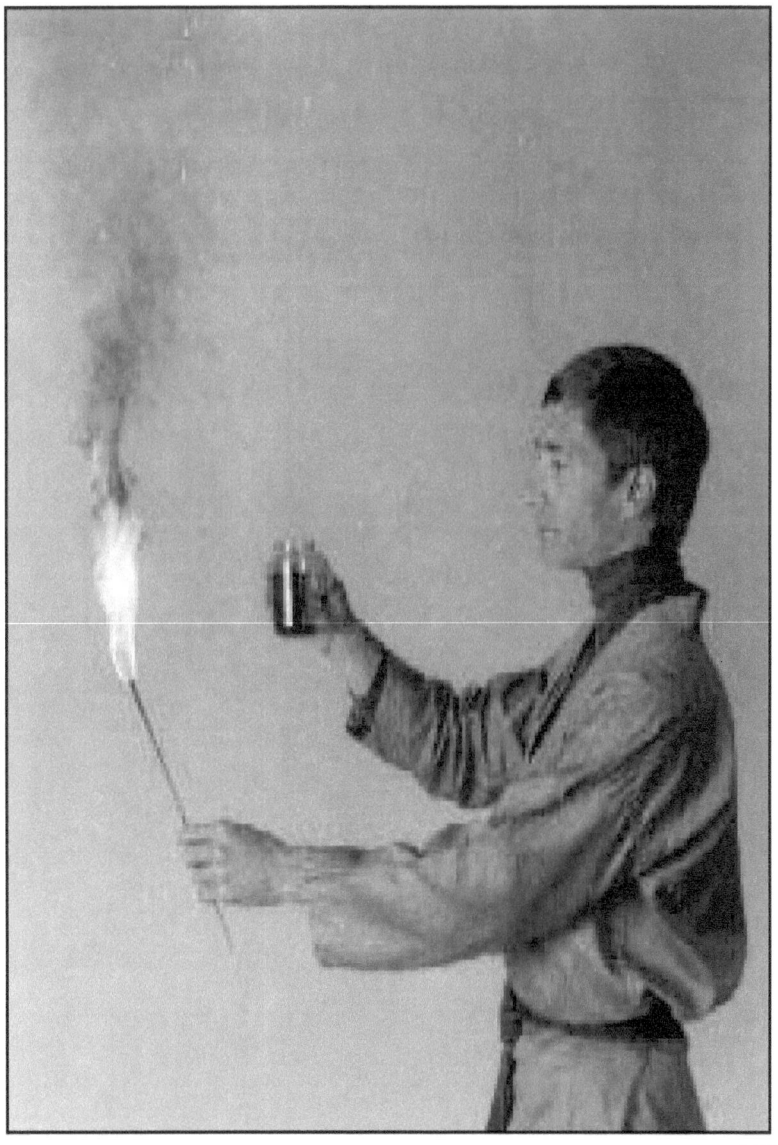

B) Keep an eye on the flame as you take a small sip of the white gas. DO NOT SWALLOW!

C) Holding the cheeks between the thumb and middle finger. The torch is held at least 18 inches from the face. Aim your spray at the top of the flame.

D) Blow a mist of flammable liquid across the top of the flame to ignite it and create the fireball.

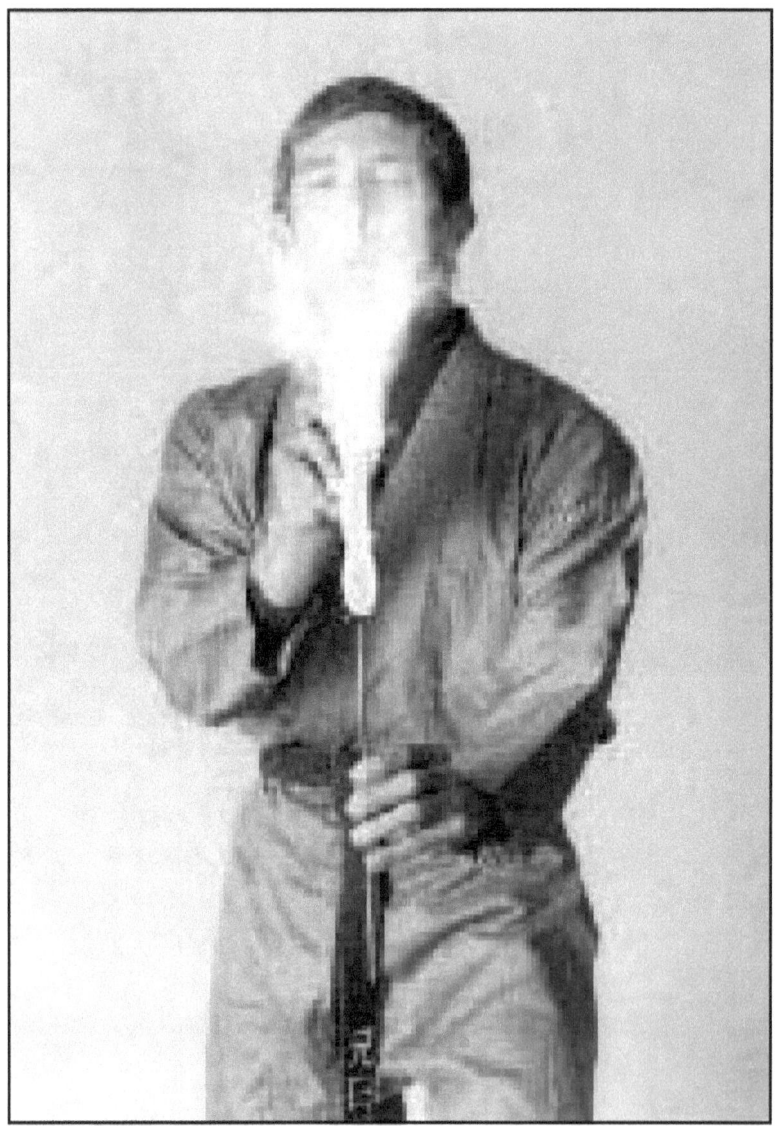

Damage to the enemy is usually restricted to singeing off his eyebrows or lashes. Since the burst of the fireball is short-lived. But, in some cases a person's hair, which if dry or sprayed with hair spray is quite easily kindled, or can be ignited.

In that regard, the use of any oils or creams on the hair should be avoided since they too are more flammable. Pop singer Michael Jackson's hair was once set on fire during a commercial shoot that included a lot of fireworks for this reason.

A FINAL NOTE OF CAUTION

As a final note of caution, we shall relate an incident that occurred when one too eager to demonstrate a skill he had not perfected happened to learn how Fire Breathing Dragon was done.

Remember that in earlier pages it was stressed that one must learn to spit water in sips or streams? Now, we can see the reason for this training. It is a practice method for Fire Breathing Dragon. It must be done. It must be perfected. Otherwise the unfortunate may occur. In Karate it is said, "After a thousand punches a fist is more than a fist."

That is because after that much practice it is an automatic action and the objective mind has control over it. In magic, they say, "Practice one thousand times before showing a trick," for the same reason. That is why we have put such importance on the aspect of breath control. Without it one may easily come to harm. Begin with a SMALL amount of fuel and work your way up.

Without going into details, suffice to say that the individual in question fell victim to over-confidence. Without sufficient practice he stepped boldly forward onto the stage and spit a mouthful of lighter fluid over a lit match.

With not enough pressure behind the stream, the combustible fluid sputtered from his lips and soaked his chin. He had held the flame too close to his face as well, and the heat ignited the lighter fluid. Even though it was a small amount that remained, it was more than enough to set fire to his face. The hair in his nostrils burned away, his eyebrows were covered in flame, and his hair caught up almost immediately. Likewise his shirt, which had been doused with the fuel when it was not projected far enough.

He tried to scream and in so doing sucked the fire down his throat. Eyewitnesses reported that there appeared to be a whirling vortex of flames spiraling inward as he gasped for breath. Bystanders and onlookers rushed to his aid and prevented him from running, which would have fanned the flames and burned him much more severely. By covering his head with a jacket they managed to put him out and get him to a hospital. Hence the damp towel as a safety precaution for the Fire Eating Trick. He had second and third degree burns; tubes up his nose so he could breathe; tubes down his throat so he could eat; and many extensive skin grafts.

Think about this before you attempt Fire Breathing Dragon.

DRAGON INVISIBILITY

It is vitally important that anyone attempting to learn these methods do so in the prescribed and progressive manner. One cannot possibly have enough control of respiration to breathe fire if one has not practiced the simpler breath control methods described previously herein.

Failure to consider the danger involved or disregard the safety considerations inherent in such a dangerous undertaking is not only foolhardy, but also downright stupid.

Even saying this, it should be recalled that the Dragon Method is not for all. So, there is no great need to master the more difficult skills such as Fire Breathing, in order to achieve significant results.

It is not recommended that anyone learn this series of techniques. They are presented merely as a study of an ancient and honorable martial art form and are not intended as a course of instruction. They are a part of the history of Ninjitsu, Kung Fu and Karate. And therefore of some interest to the true student, who seeks to probe the depth and meaning of the origins of the myths and legends associated with the Ninja. The author and publishers therefore assume no responsibility for the use or misuse of this information.

Fire Breathing Dragon Technique may be the most impressive of the Elemental Methods, but it is not the secret of true invisibility. That will be discussed now.

We have seen how man ingests various types of energy in the form of nutrients, Air, Water, and so on, even Fire. But, there is a higher level that must still be explored and considered- the spiritual plane.

Every major religion teaches the same message. Every style of *Kara-te* has as its goal enlightenment. Even the wandering hermits of ancient China, who may have seemed lost and alone, were following some Inner Path in the direction of Self-Actualization. There is a need and a motivational drive inherent in the human being to understand the universe and his role in it. Upon learning this, one strives toward perfection, which is always just beyond reach. And, one recognizes the limitless potential of mankind.

Abraham Lincoln once said, "God could not have created so perfect a work as Man to exist for only an instant. No, Man was meant for immortality."

And, this is so.

Along the Path are other Seekers, each following his or her own course. Some are at higher levels and act as Guides. Those who understand are teachers. And, there are those who have no understanding, who serve as obstacles. In a philosophical sense, however, they are merely students who have not yet grasped the importance of Lessons and Tests. That is why Ninjitsu does not kill them, even if they are violent and dangerous. Because Change is inevitable. Neither do we seek to measure the differences between these levels, but merely treat each according to its own level. For this reason, the Ninja learns to control himself so that others can be controlled by following his example. But, even to attempt such a course is not for the Many.

The wisest of ancient Chinese philosophers recognized that most people were too concerned with survival to pursue the Silent Way of contemplation and meditation. So, it fell to the Few to preserve the Art and practice it and share it with those who wish to learn.

This is why the Ninja are so vicious and savage and terrifying in war and why they are masters of invisibility. So that war does not occur. Understanding oneself makes it possible to understand others. When this happens, one is said to have compassion and mercy. The only thing good about a war is when it is over. The sooner the better. But there are those who think that violence is not only an answer, but indeed is the ONLY answer. By attacking others they bring about their own downfall.

Is it not said, "He who lives by the sword dies by the sword." And, do not the concepts of Karma and the Eightfold Path teach that whatsoever we send into the lives of others will come back into our own three times?

Is it not obvious when all religious sects have some interpretation of the phrase "Do unto others as you would have done unto yourself," that this is the Way of Peace Harmony, and Universal Brotherhood?

If we are harsh with ourselves are we not hard on others, expecting them to conform to our idea of perfection? But, is we are gentle and have confidence in ourselves, can we not trust others? And, discover that the "wonder of the Universe is in its infinite diversity and the ways those differences combine to create meaning and beauty."

The Quest for invisibility is only one road that leads to the top of this mountain of knowledge. But, it is the same as all the others. With the same chants, guidelines and particular symbols that serve as signposts and mile markers along the way in the gradual process of perfecting the Self.

Dragon invisibility is the ability to "call upon your anger" to "unleash the demon" within your warrior heart. In tactical combat this expresses itself as overwhelming force. Strike hard, strike fast, no mercy. But, the true warrior wins without fighting. All that is required is to let the enemy see the Dragon within and freeze him with a look. Practice this by imagining that you are breathing fire at the enemy. Fix his gaze and focus on his Third Eye. If your facial expression is sufficiently terrifying, he will "feel the heat" of your Will and be overcome. With a little practice, one need only "narrow the eyes" and project the thought to his mind, to halt him instantly. This is what the *Kahuna* (shamen) of Hawaii mean when they say you can see a flash of red in the eye of a wizard.

When this is accomplished, one becomes a mystic-warrior. One who can fight or disappear, a Ninja...

The Book of AIR

"He possessed the power to cloud men's minds and become invisible..."

Maxwell Grant- *The Living Shadow* 1929

THE BREATH WEAPON

In his book *Secret Fighting Arts of the World*, author John Gibley tells the story of a master of the martial arts who had the secret of knocking out his opponent with an attack of Halitosis! This man, he claimed, had long ago decided that he was not one for physical confrontation and so devised a method of creating and retaining in his bowels a particularly putrid odor, guaranteed to bowl over the strongest man by overloading the olfactory lobes of the brain. These are located directly above the nose, virtually unprotected from this type of attack. Hence the profound effect of tear gas, mustard gas, Adamcite, and other airborne agents. The olfactory lobes actually extend out from the underside of the brain and are almost like insect antennae when seen in dissection.

Gilbey, not detecting any offensiveness on the part of this individual asked him to demonstrate. Whereupon the master belched in the face of the author who promptly passed out.

In many ways this is similar to the Blow-In-The-Face technique, except that relies on tactile stimulation of the eyelids. Whereas this one acts directly on the nervous system.

For those individuals whose education was so limited in childhood that they did not learn how to belch on command, we include the following technique known in Chinese medicine as Swallowing Air, and is used to expel noxious gases from the stomach that may result from contaminated food or poor digestion. Since the stomach is inflatable, being a Yin or hollow organ, take a deep breath and swallow, or inhale while swallowing, to fill it with air. The Hiatal Sphincter at the level of the solar plexus is the constricting muscle that prevents the contents of the stomach from regurgitating during digestion

It is also this stricture that traps gases in the stomach that are produced by the chemical reaction of foodstuffs and digestive acids. Heartburn is a condition resulting from an overproduction of such gases and pressure on the Hiattal area. As sufferers will attest, a good belch will often relieve this pressure and the pain will subside. To practice burping, gulp down a carbonated soft drink and regulate the amount of gas expelled each time by gently tensing the belly.

Dragon Breath is a technique not unknown is the wrestling arena. Furthermore, in gladiatorial times, some contestants would purposely not bath for days prior to a match, making it unsavory to grapple with them. Relying on this psychological advantage, some lived on to win freedom, if not popularity.

In the same way using distasteful oils and foul smelling necklaces of garlic inhibit an enemy's aggressiveness because he is uncomfortable or unfamiliar with this type of an attack.

It is worthwhile to practice belching technique even if one has no wish to develop the chemical formula that goes with it. Since it will be needed in the final stage. The Book of Wood.

SILENT KIAI

In Karate at the conclusion of the *Kiai*, the abdomen is taut and most of the air has been forced out of the lungs by dynamic tension. In the same way, learning how to expel a ball of air from the abdomen makes it possible to snuff out a candle from a much greater distance than by blowing on it. This is accomplished by holding the mouth open in the same manner as used to "shout out" a candle rather than pursing the lips as in the first method.

Stand facing the candle at arm's length in a Horse Stance with your mouth open. Inhale deeply, tighten the belly and project the Qi at the flame by sharply contracting the abdomen. This will send out larger amounts of air than would puffing through the lips with the diaphragm.

In martial arts, this is called the *Silent Kiai* or Dragon Breath. It is considered a "gas" attack, thus it's classification with the Air Element.

DRAGON BREATH KIAI

A) Practice this form of *Haraki* standing in a Horse Stance with fists on hips. Inhale deeply into the lower belly.
B) Open the mouth and expel a ball of gases from the Hara with a single sharp tensing of the belly rather than a stream or column of air. Do this imagining the syllable "Haa…." As before, making no audible sound. This is a function of the mind and the imagination. Both symbolized by the Air Element.

NINJA MIND CONTROL

The "power to cloud men's minds" is the goal of the Dragon Style Invisible Fist. To "put the idea of Fear into the mind of the enemy" and make him reconsider his acts without resorting to physical force or restrain him to make him more reasonable.

To accomplish this the Ninja looked to the next element, Air. The Sky Dragon techniques include jumping and flying kicks seen in other martial arts styles, as well as circular fist techniques based on the wing-flap action of the flying dragon and the Poison Gas Breath, described earlier in this section.

The primary symbolism employed, however, is that of Air representing the Mind. For that reason, the techniques of *HsiMenJitsu* ("sigh-men-jit-su") the Way of the Mind Gate, are classified and taught at this level. They include psychology, hypnosis and illusion.

Bear in mind that the Chinese dragon is much different from the European version. The latter was always guarding virgins or gold or both- items for which he had no use whatsoever-usually at the behest of some evil wizard.

While in Chinese astronomy, the constellation known as Red Dragon, a sign of coming rains and rebirth appears in the night sky every Spring. In Ninjitsu the term "riding the wind" refers to the various exercises used to develop telephathic abilities of the Sky Dragon.

HYPNOSIS

The best opportunity for using this technique is during a group discussion of Ninjitsu or psychic power when the mood is already established. Select a volunteer from the group. Sit quietly for a moment to create a relaxed state. Then simply tell the subject that when you say the magic word, or cue, he will be in a relaxed, trance-like state for a few seconds and will not see you move out of his line of vision. When the subject blinks and comes out of this post-hypnotic suggestion, the Ninja seems to have vanished before his very eyes!

Of course, onlookers are treated to the show and are amazed at the effectiveness of the technique. Notice that no magic power is alluded to in the hypnotic state, only a simple instruction, usually less than nine words and seldom more than three.

The subject, like many who participate in stage hypnotism acts, may later claim that he was just "going along with the gag." But, the technique was nonetheless effective and is a crowd pleaser.

After all, why should the subject go out of his way to make the magician look good? Perhaps because he too believes on some level that the Ninja has some secret power and that if he plays along he may gain same insight into this greater mystery for himself. Thus, it becomes a matter of enlightened self-interest.

This is like another "mental" trick in which an unprepared spectator is asked onstage and told to choose a card from a display. A prediction of which card will be chosen has been previously written down and recorded. When the spectator goes behind the display table to make his choice, he sees that one card is lying on top of a dollar bill. Guess which one he will pick!

Could it be that he is actually powerless for the moment to prevent the "command" sent to him by the mentalist? If that is the case, then any later claim of denial is actually a defense mechanism designed to "save face" and self-esteem. To be sure, it is as plausible explanation as any other.

For the Ninja, it matters not one bit! Regardless of which explanation is true, as long as it is an effective technique, it should be studied, evaluated, and experimented with. Just the ability to mentally transmit the command *Blink!* would be enough to let the Ninja escape. And, among the Wind techniques of the Ninja such tricks as the Mind Whip and Blank Wall Meditation, based on the same principle of suggestibility, are included.

THE TRANCE

Like all physical techniques, mental ones require a certain amount of practice and preparation. Hypnotism is only one such tool in the Ninja arsenal.

The Subject and the Ninja sit facing each other in *Seiza*, the Kneeling Meditation Pose. The Ninja fixes the gaze of the Subject and has him take a few deep breaths in harmony with him to develop a feeling of rapport and relaxation The Ninja speaks in a soft, hypnotic tone, speaking only to the Subject and ignoring any outside distractions. This cues the Subject to do likewise.

The Ninja places suggestions of relaxation and sleep in the mind of the Subject. He does this using alliteration, emphasizing certain sounds and syllables. In this case the same one used to dispel fear, the sound of the Air Element, the "Shhh…" or Wind Breath sound. He likewise harmonizes his breath to that of the Subject, then slowly changes the pattern to one of slow, deep, relaxing respiration.

A) The Subject and the Ninja sit facing each other in *Seiza*, the Kneeling Meditation Pose.
B) The Ninja places suggestions of relaxation and sleep in the mind of the Subject.

C) With a simple hypnotic gesture, the Ninja has the Subject close his eyes.

D) Having closed his eyes, he is now dependent on the Ninja for direction.

With a simple hypnotic gesture, the Ninja has the Subject close his eyes. Note that the downward action and the proximity of the fingertips to the subject's fact, as well as the rapport and avoidance of outside distractions, not only to induce but virtually compel him to comply with the simple command. The subject is now, technically, in a light trance.

He has not yet psychologically demonstrated his trust in the Ninja not to injure or embarrass him as long as he participates in the experiment. Having closed his eyes, he is now dependent on the Ninja for direction. He closed his ears when he began ignoring distractions. Now he must "feel" his way and depends on the Ninja to guide him.

The Ninja then performs a simple test to insure that he Subject is "hypnotized" and to demonstrate to the onlookers that the Subject is "under his spell."

Psychologically, this is when the Subject "proves his loyalty" by following orders without question. Of course, he would not have volunteered in the first place unless he was willing to participate. Unless it be as a trap to embarrass the magician.

The Ninja could be directing him to put his hand in a fire. He cannot see, so he does not know what he is doing. Nevertheless, he trusts the Ninja achieved through the suggestibility stage, and so will now obey simple commands. This is a powerful position of trust and should NEVER be abused. To do so is to invite misfortune.

The Arm Levitation test determines the degree of compliance of the Subject. Specifically, he will be raising and lowering his arm on cue. But, the Ninja first makes him aware of the coming command and builds up to it slowly with his suggestions of the Subject's arm (right or left) feeling light. This can be easily suggested if the relaxation exercise also suggests that the body feels light. Then the Ninja gradually suggests that it is so light that it is floating.

E) The Arm Levitation Test determines the degree of compliance of the Subject.
F) Raising and lowering the arm on cue.

"In fact, you can almost feel it floating now…it is so light that it IS floating…don't resist it…let your arm lift upward…slowly…carefully…easily…" He continues until the command is obeyed, or the Subject breaks off, no matter how long it might take. All warfare, even mental, is a matter of stamina.

When everyone is satisfied that the Subject is hypnotized, give him praise for relaxing and letting his arm float, which rewards the effort, and then suggest that his arm is returning to normal now, that it is normal and let it settle back to his side.

After placing the post hypnotic suggestion in the mind of the Subject, that he will return to the trance and not see anything for five seconds when he hears the cue-word, the Ninja directs him to forget all memory of the hypnotic state until a specific cue is given. He then awakens the Subject by counting up from one to three or by clapping his hands softly.

One safety precaution usually inserted near the beginning of the hypnotic trance is that the Subject will fall into a light sleep from which he can be awakened any time by touching him on his left shoulder. If need be he can be roused by gently shaking his shoulder.

Upon ending the trance the Ninja questions the Subject to insure that he will obey the post-hypnotic suggestion by a) pretending that the entire experiment was merely a relaxation exercise and eliciting a verbal response. That impresses the Subject into going along with the lie. Again, "proving " the psychic power of the Ninja/Hypnotist and insuring that the subject will continue to "play along." Or, b) by thanking him for his participation and eliciting a verbal response that he feels better and more relaxed than before. Either summation may be employed. The Key is for the Subject to agree with what the Hypnotist says even after the "trance" has ended."

G) The Ninja places the post hypnotic suggestion in the mind of the Subject.

H) The Ninja awakens the Subject by snapping his fingers or softly clapping his hands.

CLOUDING THE MIND

The Ninja congratulates the Subject on his success and performance and tells him the experiment is concluded. They may now stand up.

THE CUE

After being seated for even five minutes you may find that standing causes a sudden feeling of light-headedness as the heart must accelerate to pump blood higher to the head, and the blood that was "squeezed" out of the legs by kneeling must be replaced. So, one should stand up slowly. This, however, is an excellent opportunity to take advantage of this momentary mental confusion and cue the Subject because his vision will already be somewhat dimmed and the blood rushing to his head will disorient him. Also, the quicker the cue is used, the more likely it is to be effective. The longer you wait, the greater the chance he will forget it or stop waiting for it. Furthermore, the rapport that was established during the trance is still in effect to some degree, although this too fades with time.

VANISHING IN PLAIN SIGHT

The Ninja gives the subject the same visual cue used to have him close his eyes, that of wiping the hand downward in front of his face. Unlike using this gesture to make him blink so you can duck away as in a previous technique, the gesture to "close the eyes" may be used at a great distance, since the intention is to confirm his compliance to the verbal contract rather than physically compel him to blink by proximity of the hand to his face.

A) The Ninja gives a visual cue.
B) Followed by the verbal cue.

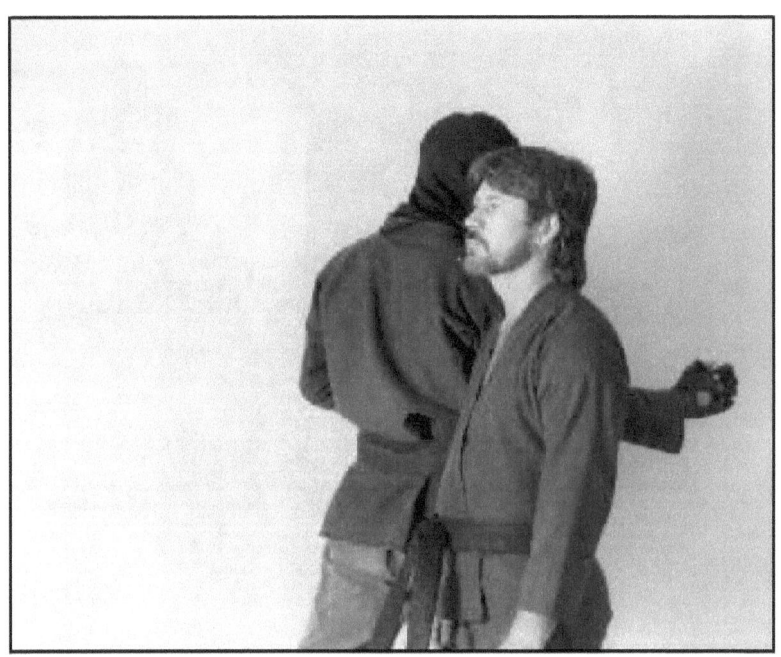

C) Cross stepping in front with the right leg the Ninja,
D) Vanishes behind the Subject before he can open his eyes

E) The Ninja remains invisible behind the Subject.
F) Suddenly making a dramatic appearance.

Next he gives the verbal cue, which is stronger and for which the subject was prepared through the hypnotic gesture, and returns him to the Trance. The verbal cue may be a simple word suggestion like "Sleep…" Or, may be a "magical"/nonsense word like "Afghanistan Banana Stand" or other gibberish that would not ever be heard in the "real' world. Such a magical word would be suggested to the Subject during the trance state.

The hypnotic trance-like state is indicated by the fixed gaze of the Subject. Remember, the blood is rushing to his head, his vision is blurred and he may be slightly off balance. He is given the preparatory command, then the command of execution for a test he did not expect so quickly. His eyes are still open, so they may "roll" out of focus as he stares blankly ahead, unmoving, which gives him a chance to recover his senses. He may or may not actually "see" the movement of the Ninja as he steps out of sight behind him. But, he does not move or react because that would violate the verbal contract entered into when he volunteered.

The Subject, acting on the post-hypnotic suggestion returns to full wakefulness in accordance with the secret instruction given him by the Ninja and looks around in search of the Ninja, who appears suddenly to have vanished.

The Subject will not see the Ninja again until he wishes to re-appear, gives the next cue if there be one, or steps into view dramatically. Thus, concluding the demonstration.

Finish with a bow to the Subject which he may or may not return. Your way of thanking him for his cooperation. "Also bow to the audience so they will know you are finished and can applaud..." Old Magician Saying.

Thus you have taken another step in learning the "power to cloud men's minds." The fifth level, the Book of Wood, will enable you, without the hypnotic ritual, to project a mist or fog into the mind of any foe so that you will be invisible to the eyes of men and genii. There is, however, still a bit more to learn about Air.

THE VOLUNTEERS

Magicians and Mesmerists are quite fond of making magical passes over the body and directing its energy with their hands. Some of this is showmanship and misdirection. Hypnotists use visual cues and directions, while faith healers maintain that a subtle magnetic field surrounds the body and that this field may be manipulated by the electrically charged palms or fingers of the physician.

In the case of actual stage hypnotism, the master of the mystic arts selects a group of volunteers from the audience. Most of these people are extroverts who enjoy participating in events for which they can receive applause. Shy people don't volunteer and are seldom even coaxed onstage. Nor should they be, because their own self-consciousness will contribute to clumsiness and a half-hearted effort.

It should be recalled that the stage is the "home court" of the magicians. While the average theatergoer is relatively uncomfortable there. This, together with the preconceived notion that the performer is somehow endowed with mysterious powers, combines to create the impression that the magician has control of the situation in the minds of the viewers and participants. This is, of course, true. He is in command, partly because he chooses to be, partly because he chooses the volunteers. And, it doesn't take but once to spot a smart-aleck looking to upstage you.

Upon this pool of volunteers he performs a series of simple tests to determine if they will follow his directions and which obey the best. If they compete with him they are "allowed" to go back to their seats and enjoy the rest of the show. From the remaining group, he selects a few who will play the part of clowns and actors at his stage direction. He then puts them through a set of simple commands designed to entertain the audience and let the players have a bit of fun.

Almost always the hypnotist states at the outset, "I will not injure or embarrass you in any way, as long as you assist me in this demonstration of the hypnotic art." This is a verbal contract to which both agree. The hypnotist then gives the person his permission to act silly, dance, sing, react to imaginary heat or cold, withstand tests of strength, pain, and leverage, or impersonate famous personalities. The hypnotist must be able to deduce which of the volunteers are able to do this and which celebrities they can imitate.

The permission to do this is conveyed to the audience by the hypnotic pass, waving the hands before his eyes, verbal suggestion, speaking in a low monotonous voice or counting backwards. All may be used and all contribute to the rapport between the hypnotist and his subject(s).

The audience is vicariously relaxed as well, since each person theoretically empathizes with one of more of the players and because they also hear the suggestions of relaxation and sleep. This puts them in a receptive mood to believe what is said onstage. It is what is known as "suspension of disbelief." The audience agrees not to look too closely for flaws and allows itself to be amused by the antics of those who have surrendered their will to the stage director or hypnotist.

Actually, when questioned later, almost every one of the volunteers will claim the he or she did feel a bit relaxed but never really felt under a spell of any sort. They were just "going along with the gag. But, some of the others were really under." Whether this is true or not is always debatable, since the effect is the same either way. It really makes no difference because the goal was to put on a good show and if everyone believed he was "hypnotized" then so much the better.

The only real danger lies in using volunteers who try to steal the show by upstaging the hypnotist. This can lead to a verbal, even physical, confrontation. But, the usual result is that the smart-aleck makes faces and mocks the hypnotist behind his back. At the very least it is disruptive, although it can be entertaining.

The magician or hypnotist usually awakens his volunteers with a snap of his fingers. If their eyes are closed, this is an auditory signal to open them. Of course, he tells them what to do verbally beforehand and may even count upward from one to three so that they are not startled by the sound. If the eyes are open, this is the signal for them to blink, giving the impression of waking up from a nap or light sleep. All this adds to the illusion of having psychic control of the subject's mind. When, in reality, it is a series of simple stage directions and psychological leverage.

FINGER SNAPPING DEFENSE

To the Ninja, the self-defense application of this technique lies in snapping the fingers in the face of an opponent or attacker to make him blink. The eyes have the most sensitive nerve endings in the body. Much of the nervous system is devoted to responses that protect the head and eyes. Blinking when a sharp sound is made near the face is only one of them.

The aggressor makes a threatening or dominating gesture. From this range he could easily use a Single or Needle Finger poke to your eye, which is as good a blinding technique as any given here. Boxers sometimes use the thumb of their glove to blur an opponent's vision by "thumbing him in the eye" from this distance.

A) The enemy makes a threatening gesture.

Deflect the attacker's hand. Do not slap it away, as this would be an escalation of the confrontation. Simply swing your hand upward at moderate speed with your fingers in a preparatory position to snap until they come into his line of vision at about nose level. In Shotokan Karate, this is called a Shoulder or Middle Block. Snap the fingers as close to his nose as possible. The idea is to get as close as possible to the target without appearing to be a threat. Note that until this moment you were still out of effective striking range.

Immediately turn your hand palm down and stab your index and middle fingers into his eyes to blind him with the Two Dragons Seek the Pearl Technique, also known as the Finger Jab. Do not stiffen your fingers. It is unnecessary and may cause injury to the user as well as the aggressor.

B) Deflect his arm and raise the fingers to eye level.

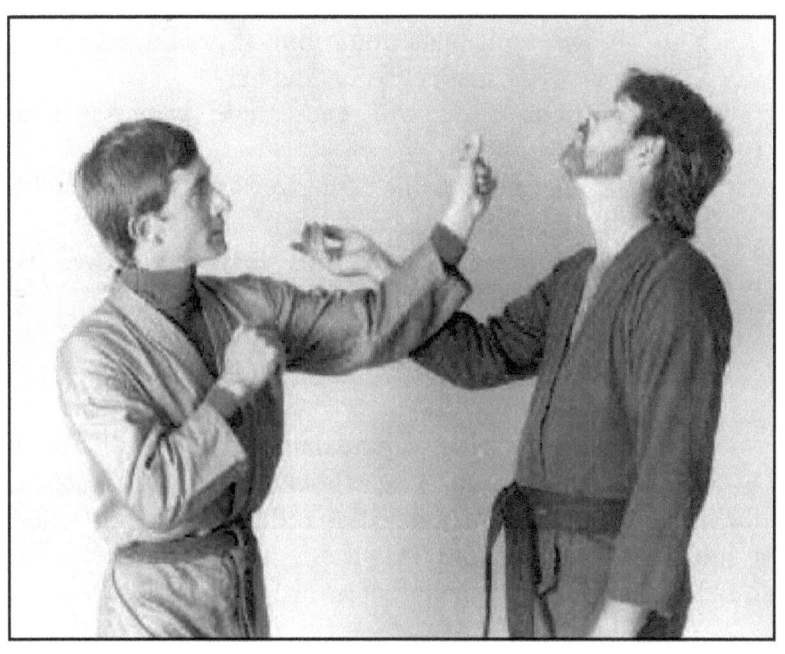

C) Snap your fingers as near his face as possible.

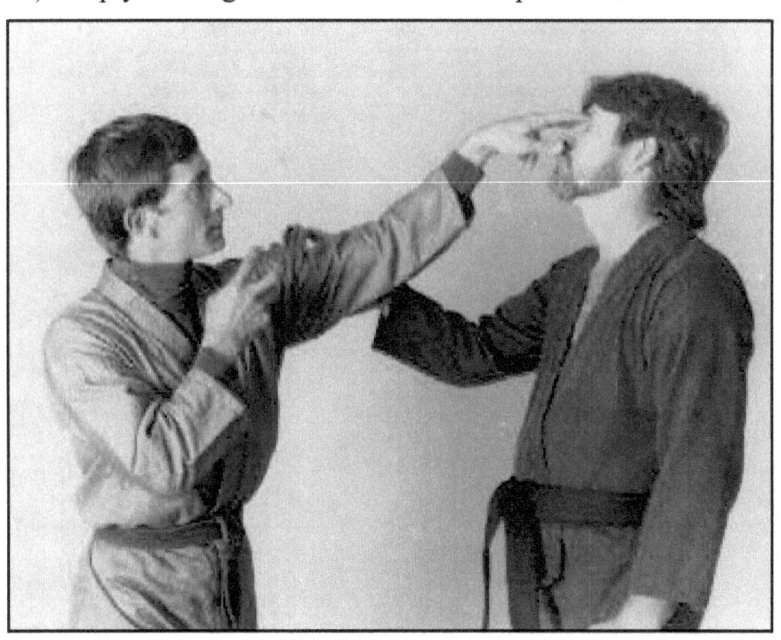

D) Invert the palm and stab with the fingertips.

- A miss will make him blink if he did not do so when you snapped your fingers.
- A light blow will cause eye watering and temporary pain.
- A poke will do the same, plus cause shock and trauma to the eye.
- A stab accomplishes all of the above as well as lacerations from the fingernails.
- A thrust causes dislodgement or collapse of the eyeball.

Withdraw your hand immediately.

For the technique to be effective, one must practice ducking out of sight as soon as this reflex is elicited. Better to look back and see how badly he is hurt when safely out of range-depending on the threat level.

E) Escape while he is blinded.

THE EYE FLICK

A technique based on the same involuntary blink response is the Eye Flick. This was first introduced to the American public on the TV show *Longstreet*, starring James Fransiscus as the title character.

During several episodes, the famous martial artist Bruce Lee was a guest star. He was introduced as a Kung Fu expert to whom Longstreet turned to learn self defense after he was badly beaten up by a dock worker. Mr. Longstreet, a New Orleans attorney, had been blinded by a bomb but continued to right wrongs and punish evil-doers.

Lee showed him a variety of techniques, throws, takedowns, knees and elbow strikes that could be used by one so handicapped. All honed and practiced as much as possible in one sixty-minute drama, and all tailored for use by a blind man.

The one technique Longstreet refused to use was the Eye Flick. He would not endanger the opponent's sight since he had lost his own.

He did eventually settle the score with his adversary, returning to the harbor to look him up for a rematch.

After a few false starts he was "forced" to use the Eye Flick to save himself and win. But he did win!

The lesson is that at the time and place where you make such a stand, if you ever have to, you must determine how much force is required and be desperate enough to use it to survive. And, realize that whatever you did must have been the "right thing" to do because it is what you did at the time and cannot be undone.

Stand with your shoulder toward the opponent in the Hidden Fist Stance given in the second chapter so you present a smaller target, left palm covering right fist as though the right will be the weapon. This is a follow-up to the alternative method of delivering the Buffalo Knuckle or Phoenix Eye Fist.

When the enemy punches, deflect his arm by shifting or stepping diagonally forward and letting it strike your lead shoulder. This puts you in range for striking with your lead hand. Note that this is the opposite of the Water Step (diagonally backward). This is diagonally forward off the line of engagement. Thus Water and Air are both "circular" in nature while the Earth and Fire Steps are linear. Swing your left hand out and around as when using the Hand Flash. Note that in that example the enemy threw a left punch while in this one he throws a right. Observe that this is virtually the same technique against both punches. The only difference being that this strike is "inside" his defense instead of "outside," blocking his attack downward. The wrist is bent as in the Kasumi Method with the fingers hidden (curled back out of sight), forming the Chicken Neck Fist, which uses the back of the wrist for blocking and striking.

Suddenly stop the arc of his left arm and flick the backs of your fingertips to strike his eye from the side. This is much less likely to cause injury, but guarantees that he will blink. This may be used as a probing attack jab or a vanishing technique, or followed up with the stunning Phoenix Eye Fist, or used simple to make him blink so you can duck out of sight.

Note also that both of these principles are circular in nature, in keeping with the symbolism of the Five Element principles. As is customary, the practice method is Snuffing Out A Candle with the Hand-Whip or Eye Flick.

A] *Mi Chuan* or Hidden Fist Stance

B] Step in aiming the wrist at his face

C] Snap the fingers sharply to strike his eyes and face

145

The Eye Flick is difficult to deflect or block because of the sudden acceleration of the fingers. Like cracking a whip, all the motion of the arm is transferred to its tip, providing a sharp snapping motion. Since this is initiated at a range of about three inches, it is much to fast to see. Hence the saying, "the hand is quicker than the eye." One-fiftieh of a second to blink is pretty fast.

Let the recoil of the finger whip bring the hand back even faster than it was whipped out, safely out of range and prepared to lash out again if need be, or launch the real attack. This motion is exactly like the Karate *Backfist*, in which the strike is delivered with the backs of the first two knuckles. The popping, snapping motion of the punch is so deceptive that it is forbidden in the professional Boxing ring.

Although Muhammed Ali used it extensively as a sort of swatting, brushing jab. Not only to confuse his opponents by making himself hard to see, but also infuriating them by constantly rubbing his glove in their face. Even though these punches did not score points or have a telling effect, they were, nonetheless, excellent examples of using the Invisible Fist.

FLICKING OUT THE CANDLE

The practice method is flicking out the candle. By this time, having developed this skill with several other fists, you will find this one much simpler. The force of the wind generated by this fist is much larger and stronger than a closed fist. Stand with your shoulder aimed at the candle in Mi Chuan or Hidden Fist Stance. Relax your wrist and let your hand drop limply away from covering your right fist. Tighten your belly.

Strike out on the exhalation, aiming the back of your wrist at the target. With your fist closed, your hand is four to six inches shorter than with the fingers extended. With the fingers extended and the wrist curled back, the hand is eight to ten inches shorter than the full reach of the fingertips. The eye of the opponent, will see the back of your wrist and act in response to its distance from his eye in terms of spatial distance and speed, allowing your fist to penetrate his defenses deeply before he is aware of it.

Whip your fingers toward the flame, snuffing it out with a quick snapping action Punching out candles like this is known in Chinese medicine as the Scholar's Exercise. When your arm is extended but your elbow not locked straight out, flick the backs of your fingertips to simulate striking your opponent on the temple or ear. By overshooting in this manner, you virtually assure that you will at least strike the side of his nose, even if he is skilled at slipping punches.

Most people, even boxers, will react to a hand coming at their face with a ducking or blocking motion as soon as the attack is perceived. Therein lies the key to this technique. The fingertips are actually closer than the hand appears to be.

BREATH WEAPONS

One final word should be said regarding the use of the breath to propel missiles other than the green mist alluded to earlier. Notably, very short blowguns are used by some Ninja Ryu to shoot tiny darts at the eyes of an opponent. The Ninja also practice the technique of Spitting Needles by curling the tongue into a shallow trough or V-shape and placing the dart in the tunnel so formed for easy launching.

An easier method is Spewing Caltrops from the mouth, but again, these sharp little three corner nails must be carried in the mouth most of the time and always a present a danger of being swallowed accidentally. Plus, they interfere with respiration.

These are but a few of the methods used by the Ninja of feudal Japan to protect their identities. If they were captured, any attempt to remove their masks would result in the expulsion of any one of several projectiles into the eyes of the enemy. Not only making identification difficult, but also providing an opportunity to escape by vanishing.

The Book of WOOD

Thusfar we have described four of the five primeval elements, Earth, Water, Fire, and Air. They are taught in that order because this is the sequence in which they appear naturally on the fingers of the hand. In *Kuji Kiri*, the finger-knitting exercises of Ninja meditation, the initial exercise is to place the fingertips together to connect the psychic channels and acupuncture meridians of the hands for health and longevity. The pinky or little finger represents Earth; the ring or third finger represents Water; the middle finger is Fire and the index finger is Air. They are joined in that order. The thumb symbolizes and connects the channels and meridians that relate to the Wood element and is touched last. The palms are then pressed together to connect the Dragon and Tiger Cavities in the center of each to form the Praying Hands Mudra, found in every religion throughout time, even today.

Of the Five Elements, two, Earth and Fire, are considered by Chinese scholars to be linear in the direction and nature of their operation. Earth is solid, like a mountain and cannot be moved or uprooted. While Fire is an advancing, consuming force, driven by Wind, appetite, fuel, i.e. Wood. This is a fundamental concept in the Law of the Five Elements, the basis for both military strategy and Chinese holistic medicine.

In accordance with the ancient Chinese pattern of categorizing things in corresponding pairs of opposites, it then follows that the other two, Water and Air are circular in nature and this can be clearly seen by watching water flow in and around obstacles and Air blowing through open spaces. Both follow the path of least resistance, whereas Earth and Fire offer the most resistance. One by refusing to be moved or changed and the other by moving and changing everything it its path.

Balance then, between and among these forces is represented as a spiral- circular motion about a linear axis. To primitive man, who first codified these principles, the best way to symbolize this type of motion was to refer to Wood, since the tree grows upward with its leaves and branches and downward (linearly) with its roots. The point of intersection between these two vortices is the ground. Just as it is with any whirlpool or tornado, which are also spirals.

The tree also grows in girth in a progressive ring pattern, showing the circular action of the wood about its linear core. Together, linear and circular motion represent spiral motion, a pattern of the universe that is only now being recognized by modern science the electromagnetic forces of life itself such as DNA. The ancients, however, knew it all along.

Those who follow the Silent Way recognize that it is only one way and that becoming an inferno of rage is only one part of it- the Fire part.

One must also have Water, the empathy to understand why this person has become so unbalanced that he must resort, usually in frustration, to physical violence.

Also essential is the Mind Sword, the power of the mind, the Air Element, to bridge the gap to him and prevent him from injuring himself or others. Nor is Earth to be neglected. This is the physical bridge between psychological and tactile.

Wood then represents the penultimate techniques of the *Invisible Fist* system. The highest expression of the principles upon which any subject, medicine, philosophy, or combat so classified can be presented. Because it is a combination of all the "lesser" elements that interact to form the spiral pattern of the Universe.

Thus it can be seen that in the symbolic lexicon of the ancient Ninja masters, Wood represented the ultimate expression of harmony with Nature and was used to designate the highest level of technique. The expression of this is found both in the martial arts applications and in the philosophical teachings that form the foundation of Chinese medicine and meditation, the "other side" of the Ninja coin. For not only are they the most fearsome shadow-warrior fighters, but also the most efficient healers.

To develop all these qualities in coordination, the Seeker must make the Inner Journey. Only in this way can one come to "know thyself." Only then can one know the rage that all humans are capable of and the compensatory compassion to balance it. Only then will one realize that the "enemy" is only pale reflection of the Self, as yet unaware of its motivation or place in the Universe.

The one who has made this journey then has the duty to share this knowledge with ten others. Not all need it, not all want it, not all seek it.

Sometimes, however, you meet another Seeker along the Path or when he makes a challenge and you recognize yourself at his stage of development. Be gentle.

Hurting him is only a way of hurting yourself. In fact, some people lose a fight because they would rather hurt themselves or let someone else hurt them than harm anyone else. This is self-destructive; the opposite of being overly aggressive. Moderation in all things.

HARNESSING THE WILL

These techniques of behavior modification used for the development of self-confidence are not limited to the martial arts. Indeed, they are found in all self-help books on every topic from losing weight to stopping smoking.

All that is required is to tie the desired outcome to the appropriate cue and wait for an opportunity to try it out. It is as automatic as the eye blink response whereby invisibility on the physical level is achieved.

Ninja are taught that if the enemy is angry (Fire) one can fan the flames of that anger and cause him to over-commit to his attack or even become so enraged that he is unable to attack, by using taunts that play on his fears. This is considered an application of the Wind Element (intellect) to Fire (anger). Conversely, one can extinguish the flames by using Water (emotion) by appealing to the enemy's self-interest, or through expressions of sympathy and support with the counsel of patience. This gives the aggressor a way out with dignity- the path of least resistance. This system is known as the Five Feelings and Five Desires of *HsiMen-Jitsu* and is, like everything else, based on the Five Elements.

The information and techniques given here are no mystery. They are just usually so covered with promises of success that they become diluted and lost. This is the way to become the master of your fate, to have the power and responsibility for your own life instead of being a puppet dancing on the strings of the few. That is why it has been kept hidden- until now.

No matter what the goal, if one sets out for it and perseveres in a single-minded manner, it can be achieved. Anything is possible if you have enough time and will power.

You have learned many new things and acquired many new skills. After those accomplishments, few other challenges can stand in your way. For now you know that the Dragon is within you, that when the need arises you are the Dragon. You have also learned to harness your Will, to be patient, and to endure. These are not powers to be taken lightly. Prisoners of war have told of how they saved their sanity by building a "dream house" in their minds. Dwelling on every detail of construction kept the mind occupied and prevented the prisoners form going "stir crazy" bemoaning their helpless predicament. Now, you too, have this mental Fortress of Solitude.

Part of the process is the study and exploration of unfamiliar or seemingly strange realms or arts such as Ninjitsu, so that no possibility, however remote, is overlooked in the quest for understanding. Also part of this process is "creating a ritual' a set of cues, a pattern that will lead to the desired result, like the *Cha-no-Yu* (Tea Ceremony) or the practice kata of a swordsman. It should be simple and elegant so that it can be easily performed, allowing the mind to dwell on the history, etiquette and symbolism of the artifacts.

The largest part of the process, however, is in its practice. The Old Ones knew many ways of teaching and of thinking, but they were also aware of spontaneous insight gained by hours of rote repetition, it is this sudden realization that is called Enlightenment.

The internal work of ancient Chinese alchemists is often mistaken for magic. Indeed, the scrolls that describe the process of turning lead into gold were completely misread by the medieval scientists who "discovered" distillation from the Chinese.

They were, in fact, texts on the collection, cultivation and circulation or the vital life-force. Lead, gold, and mercury were symbols of the Qi and the extraction of its essence can be used on many levels. They did not refer to the actual elements. In fact, it is said that the First Emperor of China, Huang Ti, died of Mercury poisoning, taking "magic pills" that contained mercuric compounds in an effort to achieve immortality. Likewise, constant experimentation with the distillation process is probably why so many alchemists of old were alcoholics.

MAGIC SPELLS

Spell casting or ritual magic is an important aspect of *HsiMenJitsu*, the Way of the Mind Gate. One must take care not to program negative thoughts of emotions as these are harmful not to the supposed victim of the spell, but rather to the spell-caster himself. The person you wish to injure today may be friend next week. Then if he should come to harm, you will feel guilty. This is true even if one puts great store in the theory of coincidence. Which would maintain that you wished for something to happen because it was meant to happen anyway. It always comes back to haunt you, therefore, most magic spells are for self-improvement by acting out the mania that causes it without harm to others.

Many magic rituals begin with a Banishing Ritual. The scribing of a magic pentagram (Five Elements Symbol) on the floor to "protect one from demons" for example. It is not, however, any external force that threatens the user of magic, it is the creatures of the Id, his own selfishness, greed, cruelty, and so on. These are the internal dragons that must be harnessed if one is to know oneself.

Most spells have three or more components. A magic word (mantra, incantation or verbal component); a talisman, (symbol, artifact, of visual component); and a gesture (kinesthetic, mudra or posture). Some also require representations of the Five Elements. Cups for Water, wand for Fire; sword for Air; coins for Earth and the lemniscate or Sign of Infinity, a figure-8 lying on its side, to represent Wood.

Magic spells are not bestowed by supernatural powers. The only force capable of doing so is the will. Beseeching malevolent of benevolent deities is merely a request to let yourself please yourself.

Magic spells do confer magic powers however. But, these are the result of patience, practice, and perseverance on the part of the Seeker. To learn and memorize the components and materials needed, to select the symbols of greatest significance and to assemble them for the ritual experience. Obviously consultation with other experts and a certain amount of note-taking is required until one becomes familiar with the principles of magic.

Spells work in direct proportion to the number of times they have been successful in the past and the significance of their component symbols. The effective range of a spell is determined by the level of skill of the operator. The more experience and power one can generate and transmit, the greater the efficacy of the magic.

Most spells operate only within the sphere of influence- that is to say, inside the imaginary shell of energy that surrounds the body, like an aura, at about arm's length. Some spells require physical contact -touch- to be effective. Some a personal item of the object of the spell imprinted with its genetic code.

Duration is also affected by the ability of the spell caster. Generally speaking a spell once cast lasts as long as the concentration on it is held. Likewise, the amount of time required to launch such an effect, including the preparation and arrangement of the components is reduced with practice. Some spells work immediately, others take a little time.

Some spells don't work on some people. Strong emotions such as anger or fear can prevent a purely mental effort to bring about change. Love is the strongest force. A spell motivated by love cannot fail, nor can any spell overcome true love. All spells are reversible, whether by the spell caster himself or through reflection by a stronger will.

Bear in mind that terms such as "magic spell" are only words. They are not the sinister or evil techniques so often associated with magic, but merely another way of describing a perfectly natural and logical ability possessed by all human beings to program themselves in the hope of affecting a desired outcome.

THE AURA

Just as the atmosphere of the Earth is held around the planet by electromagnetic and gravitational forces, so too are the charged particles that are the products of respiration. There is an "aura" of gaseous particles around the body. This is analogus to the scent that surrounds humans and is perceptible primarily to dogs, with their more highly developed sense of smell. In some cases a malodorous smell can even be detected by the normal human nose as well.

If all this is true, then why not an electromagnetic field as well? Certainly the minuscule particles possess some charge. Simply by being composed of atoms made of electrons, protons, and neutrons. If we accept that nerve impulses, although produced by chemical interaction, are essentially electrical in nature, then it logically follows that they too must produce some inductive field that extends beyond the physical nerve itself. Every other electrical current produces such a field.

Without a doubt then, there IS an aura, and it is perceptible to some gifted or skilled people. It is alterable according to respiration and mood, as previously shown.

The purpose of the mental exercise that follows is to fill that aura with charged particles released through normal respiration but more highly charged by breathing so that the sphere of influence (aura) becomes opaque, like a clear glass filled with smoke. The effect is to render the user invisible to himself, which generates the body language and mental attitude to render himself invisible to others.

There is an inherent difficulty when employing this method. Namely, if one cannot see one's hands or feet, there is a tendency to bump into things and knock them over. For this reason the Ninja train in blindfold techniques. Those that arise spontaneously are very similar to those used by the blind.

It may seem paradoxical that moving as if you were blind would contribute to making you invisible to others. But, the psychological effect of diminishing your ego to the point where you can't even see your own hand allows you to focus all your attention on those other people and remain out of their line of sight. Also, because of this intense concentration, you (like a blind man) develop more highly sensitive applications of your other senses.

THE SPELL OF INVISIBILITY

The exercise (spell) that follows confers upon the spell caster the singular ability to become invisible at will such that his presence will not be detected by normal sight or even sophisticated sensing devices. It does not affect body mass or physical manifestation. The user still has weight and occupies space. The user can still make boards creak by walking on them. Thus, there is a need for Silence.

It does overcome the problem of H.G. Wells' *Invisible Man* who found that food was visible in his stomach until it had been digested because, as indicated above, the body is not transparent but rather enshrouded in the mist or cloud. As it is still solid, however, it does cast a shadow and leaves footprints like Wells' character.

This spell remains extant for so long as the Will sustains it. The best practice is Absolute Stillness, i.e. meditation. Even the breathing must be quieted to the point where it cannot be heard by the Seeker. One measure of how long the Invisibility Spell will last is to count your heartbeats while holding your breath.

Actually, the lungs are held empty, that is to say no inhalation is made after the exhalation that begins this test. Most people can't hold their breath for more than thirty seconds, about forty heartbeats at the rate of seventy-two beats per minute for men and eighty beats per minute for women on average. With practice, however, the time can be extended to one hundred heartbeats. The ancient texts on Ninja medicine say that if one can hold the breath for this long, one is halfway to immortality. Bear in mind that this is not intended as a means to "stay invisible" for long periods. A few moments at the proper time is the key to "clouding men's minds."

Remember that there is a price to be paid for every magical work. In black magic schools this is often blood, which is usually one of the ingredients necessary to complete an incantation. On the psychological level this is an indication of the magician's desperation and his willingness to sacrifice to achieve his goal. In Ninjitsu the price is the promise to teach ten others these mysteries. Finding ten who are worthy and capable may take a lifetime. Therefore, do not use these devices frivolously or for too long. As Well's protagonist in his *Invisible Man* and the antagonists in Tolkien's *Hobbit* found, absolute power corrupts absolutely.

Place the index finger of your right hand to your lips and whisper the syllable "Shhh..." as if asking someone to be quiet. In Chinese medicine this sound is associated with the lungs (Air). It is said that pronouncing this syllable helps to dispel fear- and, this is so.

Have you ever seen accident victims who were calmed by a comforting hand and someone whispering softly that everything was going to be all right? Human beings instinctively make this sound when cooing at or quieting a baby. Whether the child becomes programmed to the relaxation response elicited by this cue or recognizes it as the sound of respiration, a certain sign of life despite pain or discomfort, is quite likely irrelevant. That it calms the person is the important factor. Likewise, it has a calming effect on the user.

The fingers-to-lips gesture is also universally recognized to mean a request for silence. Some Mystery Schools teach that the thumb should be used. But, this places the Vertical Fist directly in front of the face, making it more of a threat than a request. This gesture can be seen over great distances and when coupled with a stern expression and stern eye contact can actually serve as a non-verbal reprimand quite effectively.

From a psychological perspective it turns the onlooker to whom it is directed into a co-conspirator of silence. All the moreso the longer he waits to disobey.

With the fingertip to the lips forming the Mudra of the Silent Way, inhale slowly, deeply and silently three times. On the first exhalation imagine the three horizontal lines one above the other. These represent Heaven, Earth, and Man, just as in the Juice of Jade Exercise. On the second exhalation imagine only two lines remaining, and on the third exhalation only one line.

At the conclusion of the third exhalation, swallow. Touch the tip of our tongue to the roof of your mouth and mentally recite a short, calming phrase or prayer using the self-hypnosis technique to reinforce the desired result.

Phrases such as "I am now completely relaxed," or "I am at a deeper level of consciousness," are in this way associated mentally with the ritual of the relaxation response. Likewise a similar phrase such as, "I am better," or, "I am returning to full waking consciousness," should be used when coming out of the trance. This helps separate the meditation experience from the stress of the day, making it a refuge and a sanctuary against the pressures of daily life. The Japanese have used it for centuries to restore balance to their lives and so can anyone who practices it. The effects are cumulative and require diligent practice at first, but the benefits are well worth the effort.

Release the mudra and form instead the Eight Channels Mudra by placing the tips of the middle fingers to the tips of the thumbs. This connects the channels of energy within the body. They are like the meridians of acupuncture, lymph circulation, or blood vessels- natural pathways of circulation.

This finger-knitting position, like all those of the Kuji Kiri system, is used to connect the systems of the body in a specific arrangement so that healing or similar facets of magic can be performed. Complete Kuji Kiri instructions can be found in *Secrets of the Ninja* and *Ninja Mind Control*.

The Eight Psychic Channels run up the back, down the front of the body, around the waist, down the insides of the arms, up the backs of the arms, down the outsides of the legs, up the insides of the legs to the Tan T'ien and up the center of the torso to solar plexus level. For this reason, all schools of meditation begin with focus on the Hara or Tan T'ien.

When you are sitting with legs crossed the mudra to unite these channels in their most efficient arrangement is to connect the middle finger to the thumb and place the palms face up on the knees. You need not think of the circulation for it to occur, although there are texts and schools that teach the conscious direction of the Force. If you merely sit long enough, you will learn everything you need to know.

As before, the back should be straight, the shoulders square, and the eyes closed, looking easily and gently at the tip of the nose. Inhale slowly and deeply filling the Tan T'ien with Qi. Imagine the flame upon which you concentrated in the earlier chapters to be a small, warm, friendly fire in the Golden Stove of the Hara, filling the body with warmth, light, and life as a hearth fills a home.

Let the saliva you swallowed as you counted- three, two, one- be the Juice of Jade. It fills the cauldron and is warmed and evaporated into a steamy mist by the heat of the internal Fire. This is the mystical essence of the Cloud. Tighten the Hara and let it rise up the spine to the skull, where it condenses as golden drops of dew, the Yod symbol of the Egyptian Tarot Deck. This is the internal distillation process, exactly like the one used to distill the essence of herbs into elixirs or corn into "moonshine" liquor. These drops of dew are the refined essence of the Juice of Jade. Although they are spoken of here in the allegorical symbolism, they also exist chemically and can be activated by mental imagery, they are the elixir of life.

THE MIST

Exhale slowly and without effort or sound. Imagine a blue-white vapor or mist which is the "steam" of the internal distillation process, being emitted with the exhalation as you whisper, "Shhh…"

Let it descend and cover your legs, swirling softly to form a haze or blanket. Feel the relaxation in every part of your body as it slowly envelops the physical self. It feels good to be relaxed, it feels better than before.

Repeat this procedure nine times, letting the Cloud build until you are completely engulfed and oblivious to the outside world, forming an impenetrable shield which is the sphere of influence, the aura, by sheer force of will, like filling a glass with water.

CREATING THE MIST

Form the Silent Way Mudra by placing your index finger to your lips with your little finger extended and the middle and ring fingers curled into the palm. Inhale and draw air into the Golden Stove. Circulate it eighty-one times using the Nine Breaths. Nine deep breaths so slow and deep that they cannot be heard, even by yourself.

Imagine a vapor being expelled on each exhalation, descending to form the mist or fog that settles about the body and then begins to rise and evaporate, spreading itself upon the wind. Imagine the cloud becoming more dense as it fills the auric egg- the electromagnetic field of the body.

Imagine becoming part of the cloud as it surrounds the body completely, obscuring the form from view. Imagine the body becoming lighter and lighter until it is carried away with the dissipating mist. So that the form vanishes completely and cannot be seen.

A) Form the Silent Way Mudra by placing your index finger to your lips with your little finger extended and the middle and ring fingers curled into the palm.

B) Inhale and draw air into the Golden Stove. Circulate it eighty-one times using the Nine Breaths.

C) Imagine a vapor being expelled on each exhalation, descending to form the mist or fog that settles about the body and then begins to rise and evaporate.

D) Imagine the body becoming lighter and lighter until it is carried away with the dissipating mist. So that the form vanishes completely and cannot be seen.

Imagine the cloud itself dispersing until it too is lost to the sight and achieves absolute invisibility becoming "one with the universe," as the Old Ones would describe it. Here time and space have no meaning. One is impervious to heat or cold, beyond the tactile level of reality, were anything is possible.

The aborigines of Australia have a great lore regarding this dream-time when you are sitting as still as a lizard on a rock and become invisible to the universe that is well worth investigating. The essence, however, is to link memory to imagination. Then one can visualize or imagine the outcome of any scenario or the solution to any puzzle. It will be presented to you in terms and symbols completely understandable, some of which are archetypal and some of which are personal.

You are your own best teacher because only you know what you need to learn, and are therefore the only one worthy to be your own master. Let no one say otherwise.

INVISIBILITY

One can move about slowly when surrounded by the Mist or Cloud, and so perform acts of the Will invisibly. Chinese sages say that the secret of invisibility is sitting so still that you go unnoticed by the passage of nature. In meditation, the initial stages of practice, this movement is known as the internal work, the healing and detoxifying of the body by collecting, cultivating and circulating the life-force, *Qi*. In a physical sense, moving about means to "ride the wind"-that is to say, let yourself move so slowly and quietly and spontaneously in response to the actions or line of sight of others that you become "one with nature," part of the background that is overlooked-invisible.

This enables the Ninja to not be seen and not attract attention until he is ready to "step out of the mist" and suddenly appear to the enemy. Silence is the key. When you can breathe so slowly and deeply that you cannot hear yourself, then you can move slowly and quietly enough to be invisible. You will also have developed the patience needed to do so.

Slowness is of major importance. Think of how movement inside a real cloud would disturb the gaseous mist and threaten to expose an arm or hand to view. Practice moving in water or imagine that you are doing so to elicit the necessary visual imagery.

Any attack made while invisible has a fifty percent better chance of success and does twice the damage since the opponent is unprepared and has no chance to defend himself or steel himself against the impact. Naturally, any such aggressive behavior negates the concentration required to remain invisible, thus breaking the "spell" and making the magician visible.

This is why invisible actions are always more subtle and employ very little force. In Tai Chi Chuan it is said that a "force of a thousand pounds can be deflected by four ounces." And, in Pa Kua Chang it is taught that "to affect the lives of men, one must be outside the circle that presses them." Both of these principles are part of the Invisible Fist philosophy. The greatest warrior prevails without throwing a single punch.

It is, of course, not necessary to merely sit and enjoy the sensation of relaxation and solitude. While in this state it is possible to effect the self healing of old wounds and injuries merely by thinking them well. This too, is part of the secret teaching of the Ninja.

There are many schools and methods used for this practice-too many to enumerate here. Suffice to say that if one tries this method, one will develop a system and a suitable set of mental techniques without the need of any further instruction whatsoever. It may help, however, to consult with other wizards or healers to save time or confirm that the methods are in fact in keeping with the principles of magic, meditation, or even prayer. If they work, they are correct. It is as simple as that.

RETURN TO EARTH AN IMMORTAL

Dispel the mist gradually by "blowing it away." Exhale gently whispering the sound "Whooo..."

This is the sound of the Earth, represented in Chinese medicine by the stomach and the spleen. It is only natural that one should use the sound symbolic of the Earth to return to waking consciousness after this mental exercise.

As the breath and the sound move away, they will gradually carry the fog or mist with them and visibility will return. One should not come out of this auto-hypnotic state too suddenly. At first, it will be hard even to sit still. Then it will be difficult to imagine the Cloud at all. But, with perseverance, patience and practice, it can be done.

It might be hard to dispel the vapor, making it necessary whisper the "who" (Hu) mantra as many times as needed to produce the fog with the "Shhh..." sound- perhaps nine.

After a while the Cloud will be more easily dispelled. That is to say, in only three breaths or one, depending on the depth of concentration. These three then can be used to count up from the relaxed state, just as counting backwards, three to one, was used to induce it. Counting up to return to full wakefulness and alertness, feeling better than before, is a positive awakening ritual that brings with it the feeling of warmth and relaxation produced by the practice of invisibility.

Just visualize three horizontal lines, one above the other. The Chinese ideogram for three, taking them off from top to bottom as you go deeper and replacing them from bottom to top when waking up.

Swallow and release the tongue from connecting the Jen Mo and Tu Mo channels of the body. Forgot about that mnemonic device, didn't you? That is one reason Ninjitsu is called the Silent Way. Because you can't speak when your tongue is on the roof of your mouth.

Then, relax by sighing or remain in a meditative sate for some other mental exercise and later on return to full wakefulness by counting the lines upward or just imagining the numbers in sequence as you rouse yourself.

As previously stated, some concluding phrase or benediction should be rendered to separate the solitary cultivation of energy from mundane reality. Some schools use "Ommm…" a sixty-cycle harmonic or its variations like "Amen." Magicians seem to like "So…" as a conclusionary remark, "So let it be written, so let it be done."

HARAKI-THE SPIRIT SHOUT

When faced with an imminent confrontation, it is often advisable to "steal the march" from the adversary and attempt to overcome him verbally or mentally before he can become belligerent enough to make an attack. As the enemy is preparing to attack, so is the Ninja. He draws air into the Tan T'ien and tenses his belly.

Using his Command Voice he shouts a single word order to halt or move, bringing the shout up from the Center and directing the forceful blast of air directly at the face and eyes of the aggressor, who should blink or flinch in response. Expand your chest, a subtle "puffing up" gesture, and lean forward slightly as you follow with a long

"Haaaa…" sound, breathing the heat of the inner fire at the face of the enemy. "Show your fangs" by baring the teeth somewhat and look at him as if the human torch was setting his head on fire. This is the Fire Breathing Ninja Technique. He should feel the heat of your breath and perceive that you are about to make a kill-or-be-killed response to his challenge. That alone may give him pause to reconsider his challenge. If he breaks stance or falls back, the battle is won. If not, jump on him or vanish while he is still trying to decide if you are insane-or not!

When using the most basic method, the *Kiai*, most schools hold that "Ha!" is the best word to yell. It is the sound of the heart. When using *Haraki*, the word is not even heard. It is the sound waves that produce the effect.

As seen in the Book of Fire, true Dragon Breath requires expelling gases and foul odors by belching. *Haraki* does not. The effect, however, of making the enemy fall back without physical contact is identical in these three methods. Punching Out or Shouting Out a Candle silently is the test of this ability.

This is an example of using your Mist Attack as part of the "power to cloud men's minds" in combat. To become invisible for surreptitious entry apply the following. From your place of concealment behind the enemy, imagine the Cloud in which you meditate building in your Hara. Tighten the lower belly and blow a puff of air gently at the back of his ear. By doing this, you can make him think an insect is annoying him and become uncomfortable. This is called *telekinesis*, touching at a distance. While he is focused on himself, you can silently slip by.

Likewise, you can project this small ball of air to other spots and cause sounds that will attract his attention and draw him off his post so you can pass. This is the basis for the Ninja trick of *Yoji no Jitsu* or the Toothpick Trick, in which a small object was thrown past a sentry to make him investigate and move away.

Another method is to "put him to sleep." Just as the Empty Hand Breath Weapon in the first chapter. This time the *Qi*, the vapor, is projected using a slow steady stream of air, to form a cloud around the head of the enemy. He does not see it or feel it. But, once you have seen evidence of relaxation from projecting the Cloud at him, you can mentally send the subtle command to "sleep…" with each breath until he dozes off or becomes so drowsy you can slip by. "Think" the cloud around his head, dimming and smothering the candle flame of is will. The principle here is to mentally connect with the other mind using the charged particles of the breath to form a bridge.

Some schools teach these methods like projecting the energy from solar plexus through the palm toward the sentry's back. Others use the finger-knitting position Direction of Energy from *Kuji Kiri* to aim this stream of consciousness from the Will to the desired effect. The test of this ability, of course, is mentally diminishing the flame of a candle until it is extinguished

In a battle of wills the flame is imagined to be directly above and between his eyebrows. This is the Third Eye Point used by hypnotists to fix the gaze of the subject.

INVISIBLE FISTS

As we have discussed, the Ninja magic techniques operate on all levels simultaneously, visual, audible and tactile. The Ninja of old, often used subtle gestures to identify themselves to each other when acting undercover.

One of these, which indicated that the agent was advanced to the level of skill that enabled him to perform this Spell of Invisibility was the Dragon Palm Fist. In combat, this gesture may be used to intimidate the enemy on a subconscious level or warn him that he is about to be struck by one skilled in the Invisible Fist. In black magic schools this hand sign is called the *Cornu*, or Devil's Horns.

It should be noted that the Dragon Palm Fist of Chinese martial arts is made by bending the middle and ring fingers into the open palm so that the index and little fingers form the "dragon horns." Note this is the same hand position used in the Invisibility Meditation and is one-half of the third finger-knitting position of *Kuji Kiri*. The thumb is bent and locked to harden the fist.

Strikes are made with the Needle Finger to *Dim Mak* pressure points; by raking downward with the middle and ring fingers that form the Dragon Claw; with the edge of the hand as in the Swordhand Strike; with the inner edge of the Palm as in the Ridgehand Strike, by hooking the thumb into the enemy's eye or mouth to rip and tear the flesh, the Tiger Claw; or by poking both eyes with the two extended fingertips, Twin Dragons Seek the Pearl.

The Dragon Palm Fist was brought to China from the Himalayan Mountains of Tibet, where it was known as the Lama Hand, the Way of the Monk. It the Black Dragon School of Ninjitsu it is called *Mi Chuan*, the Invisible Fist.

Another application of this gesture is found in American Sign Language. When the back of the thumb is pressed against the heart and the index and little fingers are extended with the middle and ring fingers folded into the palm, it forms a combination of three letters or words in Sign Language.

I is formed by the little finger extended and the thumb at the heart; *you* is indicated by the index finger which would ordinarily be pointing at the listener; and the letter *L* for love is made by extending the index finger with the thumb held at a right angle. It is the sign for "I love you" that is recognized worldwide.

It is also similar to the American Indian sign language gesture for *friend*, and to the Shaolin Salute in which the Standing Palm is placed above the left upward turned open palm as solar plexus level to indicate training in the temple. Thus, this hand sign represents the Ninja philosophy of non-violence. No one wants to harm another human being. Only in the most dire circumstances of self-defense is the use of Force permitted.

The hand-to-face gesture using this *mudra* in meditation is also a method of blocking a chokehold in Judo and can be used psychologically in battle by placing the fist on the chin and slapping oneself with the palm. While the opponent pauses to wonder what is being evaluated, or why you struck yourself, he blinks, he hesitates, and you are gone.

Lama Hand

The Lama Hand of Tibetan Kung Fu is the source of the lost forms of Ninjitsu and the secret teachings of the Hidden Kingdom called Shangri-La by some. The Lama Hand is literally the art of overcoming any opponent, no matter how large or small, instantly, regardless of the size, age, or infirmity of the defender with no physical contact. The principle is to project Qi from the forward edge of the hand as if performing an Edge Block and strike the opponent in the heart charka to stun him BEFORE he comes in range of the fist.

THE MIND GATE METHOD

If Ninja are the ultimate warriors, it is because the have the knowledge and will to use the Way of the Invisible Fist.

There are many excellent fighting systems and it is left to the individual to find for himself those techniques or styles that work best for him. To quote the late Bruce Lee, "Absorb what is useful." That does not mean that everyone will absorb the same things or that what appears to be useless may not have some redeeming value. Nor it is our intent to insult any other martial art by saying that one is better than another. Other Seekers have other Paths and there are many ways of becoming "invisible."

HsiMenJitsu, the Way of the Mind Gate is the name given to psychology in the ancient texts and sacred scrolls of the Ninja. Unlike the Dragon Method which is essentially kinesthetic, this system is almost entirely visual.

As in the Kuji Kiri mediation practice, Qi in the Small Heavenly Cycle, having been raised through the Nine Gates of the Heavenly Pillar of the spine, is circulated in the Mysterious Chamber of the skull and is directed with the Third Eye. Control is exerted simply through mental imagery. One merely thinks of what he wants the enemy to do and it is done. Whatever can be imagined can be accomplished. This is very similar to the *Tantric* teachings and the use of the dream state in problem solving exercises.

Those who vanish by this method normally do so by turning the eyes upward in their sockets to look at their own Third Eye between the brows. Those who have witnessed such a demonstration report that the room lights begin to dim. Then darkness fills the room so that only a spot of light can be seen on the forehead of the Yogi. When this is gone all is blackness-practical invisibility. As amazing as this may seem, it, like the Dragon Method is based on practical, physical laws and also operates on many levels.

Two of these should be explained. First, you can't hit what you can't see. While the Dragon Technique affects the eyes and surrounds the user with a mist, the Mind Gate Method functions by simply making it impossible to see. Masters of this art can place the idea of the fist into the mind of the opponent and excel as the skills of both hypnotism and illusion.

Second, on the physical level, the application of this technique can be as simple as turning out a light. The eye reacts to the change in available light by expanding or contracting the pupil. This takes a finite amount of time. For those seconds when this process is in effect, one cannot see clearly. In a desperate situation, knocking over a lamp to produce such darkness is permissible.

By the same token, a sudden flash of light makes the iris constrict, producing temporary blindness. Ordinary flashbulbs can be made to go off to make one see spots before the eyes without the need of a camera or other large apparatus. Imagine! A flashcube as a self-defense weapon! Yet, we all know how effective they are at making us blink or squint.

Those who have been "struck" by followers of the Mind Gate have said they see a flash of light so bright that it makes them recoil instinctively. Those who have experienced the Dragon Method can actually feel its impact. *Haraki* victims speak of pressure in the ears or a sound so high pitched as to cause pain.

THE DEMON MASK SCHOOL

The Demon Mask School of Ninjitsu holds that to present a terrifying image to the enemy is often a useful psychological ploy that may even dissuade him from further aggression. Much like the stern look of a parent when hushing a child or much like the contorted scream of a martial artist as he hurls himself into battle. To this end, they devised elaborate costumes and masks made of bone or used bright red colors or fangs to frighten their enemies.

Many of these were patterned after the symbolic costumes of the Japanese Noh Plays, which are specifically designed to elicit an emotional response from the audience. This practice is analogus to the use of skulls and other alchemical symbols by some Mystery Schools to discourage interest in their techniques. Part of the training is to release all the bottled up fear and anger produced by daily stress into the *Kiai*.

Imagine it as a ball of fire being blasted from your belly, engulfing and destroying the object of your hatred or fear. That is the Fire Breathing Dragon! It is also a primal scream, a purging of the negative thoughts and emotions and it generates the courage to stand up for yourself. If you "see" it, so will your opponent. He will feel the heat of your anger and fear your wrath. And, you will prevail.

DRAGON PALM FIST

BASIC MASK

Formed by extending the first and fourth fingers and bending the middle two into the palm.

The purpose of the mask is threefold. a) conceal the identity; b) make it hard for the enemy to read your intention; c) diminish the ego by hiding the face.

DEMON MASK

BONE MASK

This mask presents a fearful image of an open maw by using talons or fangs to intimidate the opponent.

This method plays on the psychological effect of seeing bones or skulls to scare the enemy by suddenly appearing out of the darkness.

DISTRACTION

All of these things are what a magician would call distractions or misdirection. A boxer would think of them as fakes or feints used to create an opening in an opponent's defense, some think of them as sucker punches. If this can be done by breaking his concentration, the Ninja can safely launch his attack or disappear. Simple tricks like tossing a coin behind a sentry will often make him turn to investigate the odd noise. Looking over the shoulder of an opponent gives him the impression that there is someone behind him.

In Kung Fu, many styles teach to simultaneously attack two targets, gambling that one strike will succeed if the other fails, making it all the more difficult for the opponent to read the incoming attack and mount an adequate defense.

In Ninjitsu, the technique of attacking a heavily defended passageway to draw enemy troops away from the surreptitious entry of a single agent or team at some more remote site has long been a stratagem of battle. Just as has been the trick of throwing crude gunpowder into a campfire to make a blinding flash of light and smoke.

Anything that can be used to make the enemy blink can and probably has been employed at one time or another.

It only takes a second to duck out of sight.

PATIENCE AND SILENCE

We have no fear that these techniques will be misused or perverted. Since those who would do such things do not have the patience or perseverance to learn them. You can know the secret of Fire Breathing Dragon and still not be able to perform it due to lack of confidence resulting from inadequate preparation.

You can lean the secret mudra that confers the power of invisibility, but, unless you have done all that is explained here, slowly, step-by-step, there is no way the technique will ever work properly for you.

There are things that can only be learned by doing them and lessons will also be learned along the Way. No one can tell you all these things. They must be experienced and discovered for one's Self. Thus, they are presented in the manner of self-instruction.

We want or need no "followers" no devotees, no ardent admirers. We want each person to be the best he or she can possibly be. There are no masters in the ranks of the Ninja. We believe that one should have many teachers and try many styles, the better to find the truth for oneself and to train oneself and be one's own master. Part of that is developing the self-confidence of knowing you can defend yourself-by becoming invisible if necessary.

POSTSCRIPT

We are not a club, team, or army. We are a fraternity of like-minded individuals- friends who help each other and set a good example for all.

Now that you have learned the secret teaching- the Yin, or dark side of the Silent Way- do you understand why it is called that? Because the entire system is based on the physio-psychological response elicited by placing the fingertip to the lips and whispering "Shhh…"

The secret of invisibility is silence and stillness.

Now you understand why it was kept secret? Because it is so easy! There are no gymnastics, no tumbling, no deathblows or gore. No years of brutal training under stern Sensei or paying for lessons.

Anyone having read this book can defend themselves with a handful of sand. These are methods even the most extreme pacifist could endorse. They are as non-violent as the fighting arts are savage and terrifying. Yet, each has its place and applications.

Even for the Invisible Tribe, the wheel of life continues to revolve. One will be faced with problems, obstacles, opportunities or confrontations with those who believe that violence is the answer to everything, and for them it is.

"Do unto others as you would have done unto yourself," is more than just a maxim. It is also an explanation of human psychology. If a man comes to you and wants to beat you up, that means HE, for some reason, wishes to be beaten. There are many motivations for this kind of behavior, but they are of little consequence. If he wants a whipping, the Ninja is usually capable of providing it. But, since the Ninja reveres all life and values peace and harmony above all else, he will go to almost any lengths to avoid having to fight.

In attempting to live as a superior man, the goal of the *I Ching*, the Book of Changes, and set a good example for all, he will run, hide, accept verbal abuse and slander without striking back. Only when there is no escape, when trapped, when the stakes are life and death does he permit himself to use the savage and terrifying arts or the psychological tricks of which he is capable. And then, he shines.

Some schools of invisibility teach that one must become non-descript, anonymous, lost in the crowd. It is essentially the principle of attracting no interest. They instruct that one should practice by staring into a mirror until a field of shimmering energy manifests itself between the observer and the observed. This curtain of non-interest is faint and indescribable except to say it appears, as do the distortions produced by heat rising from a road to create a mirage in the desert. A bending of light rays by an area of heated air, which acts as a natural lens or prism. Not as fantastic as it sounded earlier, eh?

The *Koga Hai Lung Ryu* (Black Dragon School) of Ninjitsu performs this feat by filling the sphere of influence, the aura with a fog or mist- a vapor that conceals the Ninja - as explained. What is seen within the Cloud, in the mind, is not seen clearly at first. The Ninja must remain in quiet places that attract no attention, lest his presence be felt or otherwise sensed. This is called *Kobudera*, the "masking of real intent."

Some say the substance from which the Cloud is formed is called *Akasa* and collects in the corners with the dust that is harvested to fill the *Hai Lan* or Black Eggs used to vanish as described in the Book of Earth. This magical dust is analogus to the "pixie dust" magicians claim is found in the linty corners of almost every pocket and can be sprinkled on objects to make them do extraordinary things.

The real trick is that when he dips into his pocket for the "pixie dust" he is also dropping off the object in question.

Like the dust harvesting process itself, the psychological effect is that of mentally gathering the Qi to fill the aura, making it opaque, as opposed to transparent. Then there are those who believe that the power to cloud men's minds can be wholly generated from within, These are the followers of the Fire Breathing Dragon School.

The first step, Kindling the Fire in the Belly is the first exercise in the development of this power. Collecting the Qi in the Center, refining it with the imaginary heat of the Golden Stove (cultivation) and letting the "steam" produced by boiling the Juice of Jade rise to the brain is always the initial stage. How else could one hope to breathe fire on an opponent and defeat him with the same energy that enables Hindu Yogis to walk on burning coals or fast for weeks at a time?

This practice confers control of the "reptile brain." The brain stem in every human being concerned with survival and response to environmental stimuli. To the Yogis it is *Kundalini*, the "serpent power" that represents sexual energy. To the Ninja it is *Hou Lung Qi,* the Way of the Fire Breathing Dragon.

THE SWORD THAT DOES NOT KILL

The quest for invisibility is only one road that leads to the top of the mountain of self-knowledge and understanding offered by many others. The same chants, guidelines and symbols serve as signposts and mile markers along the gradual learning process of perfecting the Self.

Those who seek out this knowledge do so because they think attaining it is impossible and if the could do something impossible, it would provide some clue to understanding all the other things that elude them-that are "invisible"-without adequate explanation. When they find out how something is done they either don't have the patience to do it properly or are disappointed because it is so simple it is hard to believe it would fool anyone, especially them-but it can, and does.

As promised, even the most meek and mild among you, even the most passive and non-violent can find a way to defend yourself and have self-esteem herein. If not with these exact techniques then by adapting them to your own needs.

It was said that Miyamoto Musashi, the most famous swordsman of feudal Japan had engraved on one side of the hand guard of his sword, "The Sword that Kills." And, on the other side, "The Sword That Spares Life." It would be interesting to know which face was presented to the enemy and which to the swordsman himself.

For the *Hai Lung Ryu*, it is the Invisible Fist that does not kill.

Achieve mastery over your own mind and possess the key that unlocks the secrets of the cosmos... The Ninja prevails without force or violence. With his mental and physical dexterity, he evades and confuses the enemy into submission. Ashida Kim reveals here the meditation, breathing exercises and Kuji-Kiri hand forms that will enable you to cultivate and direct your Qi, the vital life force, as well as tune into the minds of others. You too can become a true mystic-warrior who can control the outcome of every encounter. $34.95

Learn for yourself the secret methods of the feared and dreaded Ninja, invisible assassins of ancient Japan, and how their techniques are still used today for secret military and covert operations. *The Secret of the Cross Step *The Sentryhold *The Sleeperhold *The Ninja Deathlock *Commando Knife Techniques "Now the Evil Ones will know WHY they fear the darkness...because the Black Dragon Tong of Retribution **NEVER FORGETS, NEVER FORGIVES and NEVER FAILS...**" $34.95

Ninja Cloak of Invisibility originally appeared as one-half of **Ninja Cloak and Dagger**. This edition contains never before revealed secrets of using the cape in combat. As a Net, as a Shield, as a Weapon, as Magician's Scarf to enabling the Ninja to fight or disappear using the vital "Time Lag Factor" that insures complete success. Includes psychological strategy as well as tactical techniques. Now, you too can become a Shadow-Warrior, a Ghost Soldier of the dreaded Black Dragon Tong of Retribution... a Ninja… $29.95

This book originally appeared as part of **"Ninja-Cloak and Dagger"** first released in 1986. It has been completely rewritten and reproduced from original photographs so that no claim of copyright infringement can be made by the former publisher who claims it went out of print in 1990. And, who have relinquished all rights on all books published by them to the Author, Ashida Kim. The Ninja Dagger, Secret Sword, or Hidden Blade is only one weapon in the legendary Ninja arsenal. The Cloak of Invisibility is another. $29.95

Ninja Alchemy reveals for the first time the secrets of Ninja breath control- how to collect, channel, and cultivate the mystical force of Qi. Comprehensive techniques for improving control of body and mind and developing the external and internal strength that make the Ninja invulnerable to tiger's claw and serpent's fang. Lifelong fitness, greater longevity, and victory over less well trained opponents, a deeper understanding of the Silent Way . . . perhaps even immortality! . . . All this and more awaits the disciplined student. $34.95

Ninja Dim Mak, the Chinese Death Touch. This unholy science is based on the same principles as the therapeutic methods of Acupuncture. EXCEPT- they are used to inflict pain, injury or death, depending on the "power" of the strike and the skill of the Ninja. Overcome any attacker with fingertip pressure. Charts and Diagrams of the Vital and Fatal Points of the Body; times when they are most vulnerable (Law of Midday-Midnight); fistic "Hand Weapons" common to all martial arts; a valuable anatomical study, a self-defense must! $29.95

OTHER BOOKS IN THIS SERIES

INVISIBLE FIST	$34.95
NINJA TRAINING MANUAL	$29.95
MUGEI-MUMEI no JITSU	$29.95
FORBIDDEN FIGHTING TECHNIQUES	$29.95
NINJA MIND CONTROL	$34.95
NINJA DEATH TOUCH	$29.95
DEADLY GRIP OF THE NINJA	$24.95
NINJA KUMI UCHI	$19.95
SECRETS OF THE NINJA	$34.95
SECRETS OF INVISIBILITY	$34.95
WAY OF THE MIND GATE	$29.95
SECRET NINJA ALCHEMY	$34.95
MI LU KATA	$29.95
NINJA DEATH AND REINCARNATION	$19.95
DRAGON LADY OF THE NINJA	$19.95
KUNOICHI-NINJA SISTERHOOD	$19.95
AMOROUS ADVENTURES OF ASHIDA KIM	$19.95
DANCING NINJA MASTERS	$19.95
FIVE ELEMENT FIST	$24.95
POWER OF NINJA QI	$17.95
CLOAK OF INVISIBILITY	$29.95
NINJA HIDDEN DAGGER	$29.95
NINJA CLOAK AND DAGGER	$34.95
WAY OF THE SPIDER	$19.95
NINJA LOCKPICKS	$19.95
DOJO-FIRST AID MANUAL	$12.95
DOJO-INSTRUCTOR'S MANUAL	$44.95

Dojo Press, P.O.Box 209, Lake Alfred FL 33850 USA
AshidaKim.com   DojoPress.com

www.ingramcontent.com/pod-product-compliance
Lightning Source LLC
Chambersburg PA
CBHW020738230426
43665CB00009B/487